ALAMO

CONSTANTINOPLE

DIEN BIEN PHU

MASADA

PETERSBURG

STALINGRAD

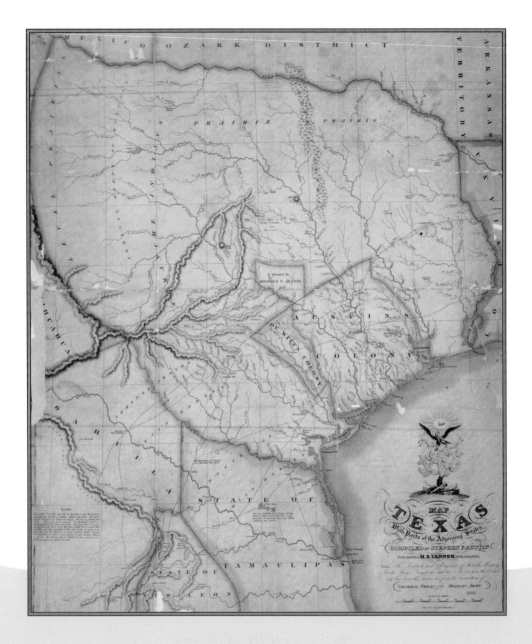

THE
ALAMO

TIM McNEESE

CHELSEA HOUSE
PUBLISHERS

A Haights Cross Communications Company

Philadelphia

FRONTIS Map of Texas with parts of adjoining states (1833).
Cartographer: Stephen F. Austin

COVER The cover painting shows the Texans' defense of the Alamo.
Davy Crockett is shown with his rifle held above his head.

CHELSEA HOUSE PUBLISHERS

VP, NEW PRODUCT DEVELOPMENT Sally Cheney
DIRECTOR OF PRODUCTION Kim Shinners
CREATIVE MANAGER Takeshi Takahashi
MANUFACTURING MANAGER Diann Grasse

STAFF FOR ALAMO

EXECUTIVE EDITOR Lee Marcott
ASSOCIATE EDITOR Bill Conn
PRODUCTION EDITOR Jaimie Winkler
PICTURE RESEARCHER Patricia Burns
SERIES & COVER DESIGNER Keith Trego
LAYOUT 21st Century Publishing and Communications, Inc.

A Haights Cross Communications ✦ Company

http://www.chelseahouse.com

First Printing

1 3 5 7 9 8 6 4 2

Library of Congress Cataloging-in-Publication Data

McNeese, Tim.
   The Alamo / Tim McNeese.
      p. cm.—(Sieges that changed the world)
Summary: Describes the historical background, events, and aftermath of
the 1836 attack on the Alamo, in which Jim Bowie and Davy Crockett
were among the many Texans killed or captured by Santa Ana's troops.
Includes bibliographical references and index.
   ISBN 0-7910-7101-4 HC   07910-7529-X PB
   1. Alamo (San Antonio, Tex.)—Siege, 1836—Juvenile literature.
[1. Alamo (San Antonio, Tex.)—Siege, 1836. 2. Texas—History—
Revolution, 1835–1836.] I. Title. II. Series.
F390 .M525 2002
976.4'03—dc21
                                                       2002012914

TABLE OF CONTENTS

The Lands
of Tejas

The old mission church called the Alamo became the site of a siege that helped turn the tide of the Texas Revolution.

For 11 grueling days, a Mexican army that numbered in the thousands had inched its way toward the century-old adobe walls of the Texas mission compound called the Alamo. Mexican artillery shells had pounded the crumbling walls of the church grounds, its chapel standing empty and roofless after decades of neglect. As the Mexicans had moved slowly forward, digging entrenchments closer with each passing day, the Texans who manned the perimeter walls of the Spanish mission had grown weary and uncertain of their fates. Now, the enemy guns were positioned just 200 yards from the mission walls, and larger Mexican cannon were on the way. The garrison commander, Lieutenant Colonel William Barret Travis, a Southerner from

7

Alabama, had sent a dozen couriers through enemy lines. Nearly all of them carried versions of the same message. It was a call for help, a plea for rescue. Yet few answered that desperate call, and the men of the beleaguered garrison began to lose their last hope. Just half a mile across the open prairie toward the town of San Antonio de Béxar, Mexican soldiers were hammering together dozens of scaling ladders.

On the evening of the twelfth day, Travis called his men together. The armed defenders numbered fewer than 200. Travis began to explain the situation. His men already understood their predicament, however. They had defended the Alamo compound for nearly two weeks, had fired their rifles from the parapets along the walls that measured half a mile around the mission grounds. It had not been enough. The enemy was still out there, still gaining ground. Everyone understood what Travis was saying. Throughout the siege, the Mexicans had placed a blood-red flag in the steeple of the Béxar church on the other side of the San Antonio River, which signified that their goal was total annihilation. The Mexicans were not prepared to take any prisoners. Before the Texas defenders lay the stark possibility of brutal and immediate death.

As Travis spoke, he began to drag his sword across the dusty ground. Again, every man present understood what Travis meant. Step across the line, Travis said, and you will remain here to defend the Alamo to the death. He had drawn a line of demarcation, a saber-etching across the pages of history. The time had come for the men inside the Alamo to pledge their lives to defend the future of a free and independent Texas.

By the 1780s, at the end of the American Revolution, it was unclear just how much of North America would one day become part of the United States. People who lived in the original 13 British colonies, situated along the Atlantic Coast, understood that great changes lay on the horizon. In 1783, with the American Revolution over, the two sides hammered out an agreement—the Treaty of Paris. Under this negotiated peace, the British granted the American colonies their independence. In addition, Great Britain ceded all of its territory west of the Appalachian Mountains and east of the Mississippi River to the new American nation. Bounded on the north by the Great Lakes and on the south by the warm waters of the Gulf of Mexico, it was a vast western territory containing many American Indians and only a few pockets of white settlers—some French, some British, and, of course, American. The future of the new United States lay in its western lands.

Few Americans believed that the wide open lands that stretched from the Appalachians to the Mississippi would be settled within a short period of time. Many believed it would take hundreds of years and dozens of generations to settle the western landholdings with villages, plantations, farms, and trading posts. After all, the British colonists had taken nearly two centuries to extend across the 13 colonies as far west as the eastern ranges of the Appalachians, a distance of barely 100 miles inland. With hundreds of miles between the mountains and the Mississippi, settlement of the Trans-Appalachian region could not possibly take place within one person's lifetime. These predictions concerning American migration to the West would widely miss their mark.

The western grasp of the new American nation would soon reach further than anyone in the 1780s could ever imagine. Hundreds of thousands of Revolutionary War veterans, many of them young men with families, moved eagerly into the western lands of Kentucky,

Ohio, and Tennessee over the span of just a few years. Before the end of the 1790s, the original 13 states had been joined by two more: Kentucky and Tennessee. Then, in 1803, U.S. lands even farther west—west of the Mississippi River itself—fell into American hands. That year, President Thomas Jefferson agreed to purchase the huge French-owned territory known as Louisiana. Comprising more than 800,000 square miles of western prairie and plains, Jefferson's Louisiana Purchase extended the western border of the United States to the eastern portion of the Rocky Mountain range. Throughout the nineteenth century, the United States would continue to look west.

Although the Louisiana Purchase more than doubled the size of the United States, it also brought Americans into contact with a new western neighbor—Spain. Spain had been one of the first European states to stake a serious claim in the Western Hemisphere. Following the voyages of the great Genoan sea captain, Christopher Columbus, Spain had claimed territories in the Americas that reached from South America to Mexico; from the Caribbean Islands to the Pacific shores of California. For nearly two centuries after 1492, the year of Columbus's first New World voyage, the Spanish consolidated and expanded their holdings in the Western Hemisphere.

By the 1530s, shipwrecked Spanish sailors washed up on the northern coast of the Gulf of Mexico, in lands that are part of what is now Texas. One of them, Álvar Núñez Cabeza de Vaca, returned to the Spanish colonial capital in Mexico City and told of the lands he had seen. Among his stories were rumors of great cities of gold and silver. A newly appointed Spanish governor, Antonio de Mendoza, listened to these stories with great interest. Driven by visions of fantastic wealth that could be found to the north, no less than eight expeditions of explorers were

Francisco Vásquez de Coronado was a young Spanish conquistador who explored the region of the present-day Texas Panhandle in the 1500s.

sent out between 1538 and 1542 in search of the cities of legend: the Seven Cities of Cíbola. Several of these expeditions, including that of Hernando de Soto in 1542, reached the plains regions of modern-day Texas. Another Spanish explorer, Francisco Vásquez de Coronado, who was barely 30 years old, journeyed across the region of the modern-day Texas Panhandle.

The Texas landscape reminded Coronado of his home country of Spain. He later described it as a "country of fine appearance." There were no cities of gold or silver, but the land did appear rich for farming and it was covered with strange shaggy beasts known as bison. Despite his findings, when he returned and made his report to Spanish authorities, he said that the land held nothing the Spanish could tap for quick wealth. As a result, Spain did not establish any significant presence in the region of Texas for the next 150 years.

Spain did not attempt any significant colonization in Texas until the end of the 1600s. Then, in 1688, Spanish officials in the northern Mexican province of Coahuila were surprised by a stranger who wandered into their frontier *presidio*, or military fort. He was a lost Frenchman, bearded, dirty, and dressed in animal skins. He explained that he was a deserter from a French expedition whose intent was to found a colony in Texas. His presence was a firebell in the night for the Spanish. Although the Spanish had never colonized Texas, they still considered it their territory. A greater Spanish presence in Texas immediately became a must. The governor of Coahuila, Don Alonso de León, led several expeditions into the region between 1688 and 1690. In 1690, he established a mission along the Trinity River of East Texas. Although

How "Texas" Got Its Name

An event that took place during the journey of the conquistador Coronado helped give Texas its name. In the Panhandle portion of the modern-day state, Coronado's men came into contact with American Indians, including a group of Caddoan Indians. These tribal peoples were called the Hasinai, but the Spanish referred to them as the "Tejas" (with the "j" pronounced as an "'h"). The Spaniards took this name from a Caddoan word, *teychas*, which meant "friends." When it was written in Spanish, the word was often spelled "Texas," using an old Spanish language style in which the "j" sound substituted for the "x" sound. From these mispronunciations and corruptions of American Indian words, the name "Texas" was born.

that mission failed after an outbreak of disease, other Spanish missions followed.

The French, however, were not going to be outdone in Texas. In 1716, a French–Canadian named Louis de St. Denis and his followers found their way to Texas and began to establish a series of missions and forts to rival those of the Spaniards. That year, they built one at Nacogdoches, on the Red River. Although St. Denis was eventually arrested by Spanish authorities and forced under guard to Mexico City, he escaped and returned to Texas, intent on expanding the presence of France along the southern Great Plains. For nearly 30 years, St. Denis and his Frenchmen frustrated the Spanish as they set up a series of trading settlements and missions.

Despite repeated challenges and encroachments by the French, the Spanish continued to solidify control of Texas. In 1718, the same year the French established their major trading center, New Orleans, at the mouth of the Mississippi River, another Spanish governor of Coahuila, Martín de Alarcón, marched into central Texas with 71 people to organize a settlement along the banks of the San Antonio River. They erected a fort called the Presidio of San Antonio de Béxar in early May. Near the Spanish fortress, a Catholic friar named Father Antonio Olivares oversaw the building of a church, the Mission of San Antonio de Valero. Additional missions were constructed near San Antonio. In time, a civilian settlement followed, which the Spanish called the Villa of San Fernando. It was here that the adobe chapel of the Mission of San Antonio de Valero was built. More than a century later, this chapel would play a signifi-cant role in Texas history and would be remembered as the Alamo.

From its earliest days and throughout the 1700s, the mission-fort community of San Antonio de Béxar faced the kind of difficulties common to those living on the frontier. Indian attack was a constant threat. In 1730, a band of Lipan Apache attacked the presidio, killing two soldiers and wounding 13. The Apache also stole 60 head of Spanish cattle. Rarely was San Antonio de Béxar free from violence and attack. Seemingly constant raids resulted in the theft of cattle and horses. Hapless victims, caught alone in the wrong place at the wrong time, were killed. The Spanish retaliated, dispatching soldiers across the barren southern plains in search of enemies who seemed to disappear at their approach. While the Apache bands were a never-ending threat, other Indian tribes menaced the Spanish in their mission settlements. In 1758, 2,000 Comanche warriors, hundreds of them armed with French muskets, swept down on the mission at San Saba, stealing dozens of horses and sacking the mission buildings. When a unit of Spanish soldiers rode out of their presidio to fight the Comanche raiders, the Spanish were slaughtered to the man. Before the raid was over, the Comanche murdered the priests and torched the Spanish mission. The raid enraged Spanish colonists across the region, especially in the capital at San Antonio de Béxar.

The future of Spanish influence in Texas was at stake. The authorities of Spain had encouraged the establishment of missions to help tame the American Indians of the region. By converting them to Christianity, perhaps the various warrior bands of southern Plains tribes might be encouraged to settle down and become loyal Spanish subjects. The mission system did not convert great numbers of hostile American Indians, despite the friars' best efforts over several decades. One mission, San Antonio de Valero, was home to fewer than four dozen Indian converts after 75 years of priestly effort.

Their small numbers caused a constant problem for

the Spanish. Texas, a vast expanse of territory, could not possibly be tamed with only a few thousand Spanish colonists in residence. By the 1790s, the total Spanish population in Texas amounted to fewer than 3,000 people. This included any American Indians from the region who had converted to Catholicism. As the Spanish residents attempted to cling to their toehold in Texas, they received little support from the authorities sitting in Mexico City, located more than 1,000 miles to the southwest, in the heart of the viceroyalty of Mexico. This was because by 1763, the threat of French encroachment had all but disappeared. In that year, the French had lost their claims to the western lands of Louisiana under the treaty ending the Seven Years' War (in North America, the conflict was known as the French and Indian War). With no ongoing French threat, Spanish authorities in Mexico City began to worry less about their distant colonial populations.

As a result, with each passing decade, the Spanish colonists of Texas distanced themselves from Spanish control and authority. They had been neglected by the authorities representing the Spanish king. Even the Catholic Church hierarchy, from Mexico City to the Vatican in Rome, had failed to give adequate support to their missionary outposts in the remote hill country of Texas.

With the nineteenth century approaching, the Spanish government found its hold on its northern provinces, from California to Texas, on shaky ground. There were not enough loyal Spanish residents to hold back the irresistible tide of outsiders as they crossed Spanish provincial borders. Spain needed new blood and new supporters.

In an effort to increase the number of residents in its northern territory, the Spanish government took a bold step in the later decades of the eighteenth century. The government invited non-Spanish residents to come to the Louisiana Territory. During the 1780s, German and French Catholics were allowed entrance into the wide open region. Then British Loyalists from the newly independent United States were invited. The Spanish believed that fellow Europeans, displaced by war and religious intolerance, would gladly accept a safe haven and a fresh start in Spanish-controlled Louisiana.

Next, in 1786, westward-moving Americans were also allowed entrance. The Spanish anticipated that such migrants would be loyal to the ruling viceroy in Mexico City. In time, the great Kentucky explorer and pioneer, Daniel Boone, decided to settle in the region of modern-day Missouri, which was controlled by the Spanish. Americans rushed into Louisiana, Missouri, and West Florida by the thousands. Then, in 1800, the king of Spain abruptly halted the flow of Americans into his northern colonies. It seemed that too many Americans had taken up the offer of the Spanish. Those Americans were fiercely independent, had no love for Spain or Catholicism, and remained extremely loyal to their American identity, despite the fact that they lived on Spanish lands.

With the barring of Americans from Spanish lands, plus the closing of the port of New Orleans to American traffic on the Mississippi River, the future of Spain's control over the region was questioned by many Americans. Then, suddenly, everything changed in Texas. Before the end of 1800, the French ruler, Napoleon Bonaparte, intent on expanding his dominance over neighboring European powers, forced the king of Spain to grant him ownership of the vast Louisiana region. In just three years, the French leader sold that territory to the United States. The purchase of Louisiana was a high point of

Thomas Jefferson's first term as president.

Over the next 20 years, the power of Spain over its North American territories began to weaken. The loss of Louisiana to the French, followed by the American purchase of the region, ensured the migration of many thousands of Americans right up to Spain's back door in Texas. Then, in 1819, Spain decided to surrender control of Florida to the Americans as well. Spanish control of the region was limited, and many of the residents were American citizens. Under the Adams-Onís Treaty of 1819, the United States government paid the Spanish government in Madrid $5 million for the strategic region, which had been in Spanish hands since the early 1500s.

The nineteenth century was presenting new challenges to the old Spanish Empire in the New World. Despite its best efforts over three centuries, the population of Spain's northern provinces had remained limited. The tide of Americans moving west was, to the small number of Spanish colonists in Texas, shocking. Between 1800 and 1820, more than 2 million Americans had trekked west of the Appalachian Mountains and spread out as far west as the northern and eastern borders of Texas. Even as late as 1820, there were still fewer than 3,500 Spanish residents in Texas. Spain did receive some assurances from the U.S. government that it had no claims to Texas and that its military would protect the borders between the two nations. Such promises were not easy to keep.

Even in the 1790s, American adventurers had threat-ened the Spanish authorities in Texas. One of the most notorious was a cattle and horse rustler named Philip Nolan. By 1800, Nolan was trying to figure out how to gain control of part of Texas for himself. He built a fort among the Caddo Indians, where he and his men set up a base of operations. Only when Spanish authorities dispatched a 100-man military unit to put a stop to Nolan's schemes did his career come to a violent end. In a short but pitched battle near modern-day Waco, Nolan was killed and his small band of men was taken prisoner. Ten years later, another American adventurer, Augustus Magee, also launched a plot to take Texas away from Spanish control. A West Point graduate and former army officer, Magee allied himself with an exiled Spanish official, Bernardo Gutiérrez de Lara, who was living in New Orleans. Between the two schemers, they recruited over 200 American riflemen.

During the summer of 1812, Magee and Gutiérrez led their men across the Texas border to a place called Bahia. (During the Texas Revolution, which took place a generation later, the site would be known as Goliad.) There, they encountered 1,500 Spanish troops, along with the governor of Texas, Manuel Salcedo. During negotiations, Magee agreed to surrender, but was later killed. His riflemen then fought their way free from their Spanish captors, killing more than 200 soldiers in the process. Over the next year, Gutiérrez continued to lead his raiders across Texas, trying to gain a foothold for their invasion. Before the last of the Americans abandoned the Magee-Gutiérrez expedition, more than half of them had been killed.

Although the Magee-Gutiérrez scheme in Texas failed, other conspiracies followed. They usually involved Americans who were bent on wresting Texas from Spanish control. In 1821, the Spanish finally met their match. Their ultimate challenge came not from raiding American invaders, however, but from the people of Mexico.

The previous decade had been one of turmoil in New Spain, as Spain's New World territory was called. After

300 years of harsh and restrictive rule by Spain, most Mexicans were ready to revolt against their colonial overlords. In 1810, a Mexican priest named Miguel Hidalgo y Costilla began to lead the fight for Mexican independence from Spain. He appealed to American Indians and *mestizos*, people of mixed Spanish and Indian descent, to follow him and throw off Spanish rule. After Hidalgo was captured a year later and executed, another priest, José María Morelos y Pavón, took up the cause, enlisting recruits and arming them with guns captured from the Spanish. Although he won victories against Spanish armies, his followers eventually turned against him because they rejected his liberal goals of racial equality and of ending special privileges for the Catholic Church.

Not until 1820 did the true revolution begin to sweep across Mexico. That year, liberal-minded revolutionaries, led by Vincente Guerrero, forced the Spanish viceroy ruling Mexico to accept a new constitution that greatly limited his power. However, conservative elements in support of the viceroy attempted to destroy the liberal movement by sending troops to crush them. The conservatives sent one of their own, General Agustín de Iturbide, to move against Guerrero's followers. The revolutionary spirit, however, led Iturbide to join Guerrero's forces in February 1821, and march to demand Mexican independence. Many people joined them—both liberals and conservatives—and Mexico became fully independent from Spain by 1821.

With Spanish influence removed, the two factions that then ruled the free nation of Mexico turned on one another. The conservatives still wanted a monarchy, while the liberals longed for a republican form of government. Iturbide turned on both factions and had himself crowned emperor in 1822. Iturbide proved to be

Father Miguel Hidalgo helped lead the fight for Mexico's independence from Spanish rule. This painting shows Hidalgo and his fellow revolutionaries celebrating their success after Mexico became independent in 1821.

an inept ruler. Meanwhile, revolutionaries in Mexico were not prepared to abandon their goals. The next year, a Mexican general who was one of Iturbide's former commanders led a revolutionary army and drove the would-be emperor from power in Mexico City. With the monarchy destroyed, the people called for a convention and the writing of a constitution. By 1824, this new framework of government was completed. The 1824 Mexican Constitution established a federal government for the former Spanish colony and created a two-house legislature and an elected office of president. For the time being, one of the revolution's heroes was the general who had removed Iturbide from power. His name was Antonio López de Santa Anna, and he would one day play a key role in the history of Texas.

Although Stephen Austin (known as "the Father of Texas") is seen here brandishing a rifle after receiving word of an Indian raid, in reality, Austin worked hard to maintain peaceful relations with local tribes as often as possible.

Gone to Texas

The success of the Mexican Revolution of 1821 brought extraordinary change to the people who had lived under the oppressive rule of Spain. New days lay ahead for the Republic of Mexico. The revolution changed the future for Texas as well. In fact, the course of Texas history was already being decided by an adventurous entrepreneur from Missouri named Moses Austin. He was one of tens of thousands of Americans who had taken up residence along the frontier in Louisiana when Spain had opened those western lands to immigrants prior to 1800. Over the years, Moses Austin had proven loyal to Spain. Then, in the midst of the Mexican Revolution, Austin prepared plans that would chart Texas's future forever.

Prior to moving west of the Mississippi River in 1797, Connecticut-born Moses Austin had operated lead mines in Virginia. When those mines failed to make enough profit, Austin decided to move to Upper Louisiana in modern-day Missouri. He had heard stories of rich lead deposits there, and by 1798, 36-year-old Austin had gained permission from the Spanish minister to the United States to explore the region south of St. Louis in search of the metal. After arriving in St. Louis, Austin, mud-spattered from his trip, changed into his finest clothes, including a scarlet-lined cape and a laced shirt. He called on the Spanish commandant, who was immediately impressed by the American who seemed to be a gentleman. After some brief negotiations, Austin received a generous land grant of a *sitio* of Missouri property—a mass of land equivalent to one square league, or 4,400 acres (1,781 hectares).

Austin's Missouri venture proved successful. He established mines, built smelting furnaces, and made money. He became a leading citizen in Washington County, Missouri.

In 1803, everything began to change. The French took control of the region, then sold the territory to the expanding United States. Now living on American soil, Austin was in a position to make even greater profits. In a short time, he was even able to found the Bank of St. Louis and make himself one of its primary stockholders. For six years, Austin served in the Missouri House of Representatives. He found success everywhere.

Then, suddenly, in 1819, Moses Austin lost nearly everything. That year, a severe depression, called a "panic," hit the United States. Though there were several causes of the national economic disaster, overspeculation in western land was at the top of the list. Many western and frontier banks, including Austin's Bank of St. Louis, had loaned money to land speculators in the hope of making quick profits. Austin's was among them. After 20 successful years in Missouri, Austin found himself broke for the second time in his life.

Moses Austin was not a man to sit still and let events control his destiny, however. He searched for opportunities on the Arkansas frontier, but decided to move to New Orleans. Even in that expansive Mississippi Delta town, Austin could only find work editing a local newspaper. Discouraged, he wrote home to his family: "I shall earn nothing to help you with for at least 18 months."

Despite his depressed outlook for the future, Austin was forming a plan. He had come to Missouri when it had been part of the Spanish colonial frontier. Now, in 1820, he looked to another Spanish-held frontier region as a place where he might find opportunity: Texas.

In the summer of 1820, Austin, now nearly 60 years old, set out for the Texas frontier. He rode 800 miles (1,288 kilometers) on horseback along the El Camino Real, the Royal Road, which was the main road that cut east to west across the region. He reached San Antonio de Béxar that fall. As he and his traveling companions rode through the town, they passed the old mission building of San Antonio de Valero, the abandoned church structure that would later be called the Alamo.

The old Spanish community of fewer than 1,000 residents was in turmoil. A group of Americans had only recently attempted to take over part of East Texas, and the local population had been left a bit jittery. Austin soon met with the governor, Antonio de Martínez, and tried to pass himself off as a Frenchman, since fear and hatred of Americans was running high. The trick did not work. Once the governor realized that Austin was an American, he refused to speak to him and ordered him out of Texas immediately. If Austin and his men even spent the night in Béxar, they would be arrested.

Dejected and knowing he had little hope of a second audience with the governor, Austin emerged onto the dusty, shabby streets of Béxar, as his Texas visions began to fade. Then, in an unlikely coincidence, Austin, who was hundreds of miles from home, ran into an old friend, Felipe Enrique Neri, Baron de Bastrop. Austin and Bastrop had known one another when they were fellow landowners in Spanish Louisiana. Bastrop, who originally came from Holland, had moved to Texas after the French gained control of Louisiana. In the intervening years, he had lost much of his wealth, but he was still a gentleman, an aristocrat, and, most important to Austin, he had the ear of the governor. After the two men rekindled their acquaintance, Bastrop agreed to serve as Austin's agent.

Within a week, Bastrop had managed to get Martínez's signature on a petition requesting permission for Moses Austin to bring 300 families to Texas for the purpose of settlement. The petition was later approved by the ruling commandant of the eastern internal provinces, General Joaquín de Arredondo. Previously, Arredondo had ordered the governor to keep all North Americans out of Texas. Bastrop was able to convince such important Mexican officials that Austin was reliable and had proven that he was loyal to Spain. Bastrop also reminded the governor and the general that more colonists would help ease the problem of Indian raids, and that since no native Mexicans or Spaniards were willing to migrate to Texas, Americans might be the best settlers. Bastrop also stressed that Anglo–American colonization in Louisiana had worked extremely well.

Even though the Mexican governor had ordered Austin out of Béxar the same day he arrived in December 1820, the enterprising American did not leave the sleepy Texas town until more than a week later. When he arrived in Texas, he was an American with his hat in his hand. As he left for home to recruit settlers for his venture, he was on the verge of becoming an important Texas landowner.

After he returned to Missouri, Austin sent word of his plan to his oldest son, Stephen, who was in New Orleans. At first, Stephen was opposed to the grand venture. Over the following weeks, however, the father tried to convince his son that a great opportunity had been placed before them.

By May 1821, word of Moses Austin's land grant arrived from Texas. Austin was to be the owner of any 200,000 acres (80,937 hectares) of Texas land of his choice. Moses was ecstatic, sending off a note to his son: "I now can go forward with confidence, and hope and pray you will Discharge your Doubts as to the Enterprise. Raise your spirits. Times are changing. A new chance presents itself." Despite his father's enthusiasm and optimism, Stephen still remained skeptical and uncommitted. He did agree to join his father on his next trip to Texas in search of a site for his American colony.

An unforeseen event changed the plans for the colony. Moses Austin contracted pneumonia and died on June 10, 1821. Sadly, he never saw the lands he had been granted by the Mexican government. On his deathbed, according to Stephen Austin's mother, Moses had "begged me to tell you [Stephen] to take his place, and . . . he prayed [God] to extend his goodness to you and to enable you to go on with the business in the same way he would have done." With the death of his father, the rest of Stephen Austin's life had been determined.

Over the following months, Stephen Austin, just 27 years old, made his plans for his father's colony. In July, he and some associates made a trip to San Antonio, where young Austin was received by Governor Martínez. He also met his father's friend, Baron de Bastrop. Within two weeks of his arrival, Austin had laid out a blueprint for his colony. Each male colonist would receive 640 acres (259 hectares) of land, plus an additional 160 acres (65 hectares) for his wife and each of his children. Austin then determined to find a location for his colony. He explored the lower end of the Colorado and Brazos rivers for suitable land. As he traveled, he came into contact with American settlers who had made their homes illegally on Mexican soil. Exploring the vast reaches of this great western frontier, Austin liked what he saw. By late September, Austin had made his decision, selecting land adjacent to the banks of the Brazos River. He made note of its beauty in his personal journal, calling it "a most beautiful situation for a town or settlement. The country back of this place for about 15 miles (24 kilometers) is as good in every respect as a man could wish for, land all first rate, plenty of timber, fine water." Austin even selected a site for a colony-based town which he decided to name San Felipe de Austin, located 175 miles (282 kilometers) from San Antonio de Béxar.

Austin then sent word to Martínez about the territory he had chosen, describing the borders of his new colony. It was a huge amount of land. With no accurate survey of Texas in existence, Austin was unable to know exactly how large a landmass he was requesting from the Mexican government. It was much larger than the amount he had been promised, comprising approximately 11 million acres (4.5 million hectares). Although his grant had authorized him to introduce 300 American families to the largely unoccupied regions of Texas, Austin believed he could find more than 1,500 families eager to make a new home in Mexican Texas.

Everything began to move quickly. By November, Austin was back in New Orleans, preparing to move to his new land grant. He was soon besieged by hundreds of requests for land from Americans who had learned by word of mouth of the new colony. Americans were eager to get cheap land in Texas. In the United States, the federal government had made a practice of selling land at $1.25 an acre. The lands Austin was about to open to American immigrants would cost less than one-tenth of that amount. Even before Austin returned to his fledgling colony in January 1822, some American colonists were waiting there to greet him, having arrived two months earlier.

Texas fever was soon sweeping America. People from Ohio to Mississippi prepared to flock to Austin's colony. Frontiersmen in Kentucky, Tennessee, and Georgia abandoned their remote farms, scratching the initials "G.T.T." ("Gone to Texas") on their cabin doors. When they came to Texas land, they would no longer be squatters with no legal title to the land they occupied, but instead settlers who had been invited by an enterprising young man who had the favor of the Mexican government. Guidebooks were printed, explaining to those east of the Mississippi River how to reach the promised lands of the empresario (land agent) Stephen Austin. Such pamphlets described the land that waited for the adventurous: "No sturdy forest here for months defies the axe, but smiling prairies invite the plough. Here no humble prices reduce the stimulus to labor, but the reward of industry is so ample as to furnish the greatest incentive." One Illinois father rushed his family out to Texas. Since each of his offspring would receive 160 acres (65 hectares), he was glad he had 11 children.

Americans came in droves, all tempted by the lure of cheap land. It was a region impossible to describe with exaggeration, although some tried. Those who arrived first encouraged their friends and relatives back in the United States to join them. One wrote: "It does not appear to me possible that there can be a land more lovely."

In his book, *A Time to Stand*, historian Walter Lord described the allure of the land that brought Americans by the wagonload to Mexican Texas:

> The sheer abundance of everything staggered the imagination. No drought or falling water table had yet taken its toll. The prairie was an endless sea of waving grass and wild flowers. . . . The fresh green river bottoms were thick with bee trees, all dripping honey. Deep, limpid pools lay covered with lilies. The streams were full of fish, and game was everywhere—bear, deer, rabbits, turkeys, prairie chickens. Mustangs and buffalo roamed at will—there for the taking.

The land grants handed out by Austin were, indeed, generous by any standards. Those who came to ranch on the rich Texas lands received 1,500 acres. Others received many times that amount. The cost was cheap. Colonists were supposed to pay Austin about 12 cents an acre—about one-tenth of the price they would have paid for the same amount of land in the United States—but often such payments were suspended.

The other terms for settlement were also appealing. As colonists, the people were exempt from taxes and customs payments during their first seven years in Texas. They were supposed to pledge their allegiance to the king of Spain (later, this was changed to the Republic of Mexico) and to convert to the Catholic Church. Most of them did so, but only in name.

As more and more Americans flocked to Texas, it appeared that Austin's colonial efforts were destined to become a great success. Then, disaster struck. In March 1822, while visiting San Antonio de Béxar, Austin received news of the Mexican Revolution. Now that the Mexicans ruled their own land, all of Austin's land grants were

Once Austin began his colony, Americans came in huge numbers to take advantage of the opportunity to buy large amounts of inexpensive land. This mural shows new colonists gathering in what is now Bay City, Texas, as Austin and Bastrop hand out land parcels.

rendered invalid. He would have to go to Mexico and renegotiate with the new government.

By the next month, Austin was in Mexico City, negotiating with the new national leaders. "I arrived in the City of Mexico . . ." he wrote, "without acquaintances, without friends . . . with barely the means of paying my expenses for a few months. Added to all this I found the

City in an unsettled state, the whole people and country still agitated by the revolutionary convulsion. . . ." Weeks passed, and Austin was unable to find the proper officials he needed to transfer his Spanish grants. Not until Iturbide made himself emperor and dissolved the Mexican Congress was Austin able to secure the emperor's signature for his grant transfer. By then, nine months had passed since Austin arrived in Mexico City. Then, just when he was certain that his grants were secure, Iturbide was overthrown and a new Congress rose to power. Again, the Mexican government's deal with Austin was dissolved. Not until the following April, after he had spent a year in the Mexican capital, was Austin able to get his grants recognized by the Mexican Congress.

To his surprise, the new terms for the grants were even more generous than those that had been granted by Spain. Each landowner would receive 4,605 acres (1,864 hectares) of Texas property; taxes were waived for six years; and Austin would be paid 12.5 cents per acre. Austin also received a personal grant of 100,000 acres (40,469 hectares) of his own land.

There were, however, some restrictions. Like the Spanish government, the Mexicans wanted all new colonists to pledge allegiance to Mexico, and to convert to Catholicism. (Officials told Austin quietly that Catholic rites would not be forced on the colonists, many of whom were Protestants.)

There were additional restrictions that Austin himself placed on his colonists. When any new settler arrived, Austin had him sign a contract stating that the newcomer was a "moral and industrious man, and absolutely free from the vice of intoxication." After 17 months in Mexico, Austin's work was finally completed and, by August 1823, the patient entrepreneur was back in Texas.

The months he was away had been crucial. The colonists

had faced serious problems, including a drought that destroyed their first corn crop. American Indians had harassed their settlements, and some Americans had packed up their families and belongings and returned to their homes in the United States. With Austin back to offer his assurances, however, the push to abandon Texas was turned around. The colony then experienced additional growth. By September 1824, Austin's land commissioner — none other than his father's old friend, Baron de Bastrop — had completed 272 new land titles and had dozens more in the works. By 1827, Austin was only three land titles short of the 300 families he had promised he would settle on his grant lands. The first 297 families came to be known as the Old Three Hundred, in recognition of their status as the original settlers of Austin's lands. Of that number, only seven ever forfeited their lands.

Thousands of other settlers followed. Who were these people who came to settle Texas? Nearly all were Americans, and they generally fit a profile, partially because Austin would only allow certain types of settlers, and he worked hard to keep others out. For the most part, they were of Anglo–American descent whose ancestors had immigrated to America even before there was a United States. They were of English, Scottish, and Irish descent. Several were Germans. They came from the United States directly, from the Trans-Appalachian states and territories: Kentucky, Tennessee, Arkansas, Missouri, Alabama, Louisiana, and Mississippi. Some came from as far away as New England. Yet Austin did not want anyone who was, by nature, nothing more than a backwoodsman, as Austin put it. He stipulated early on that "no frontiersman who has no other occupation than that of hunter will be received—no drunkard, no gambler, no profane swearer, no idler." As a result, nearly to the last man, woman, and child, Austin's colonists were farmers, hardworking, honest, upright, moral folks. Nearly all were educated to some extent. Only four of Austin's original Old Three Hundred could not read or write. Austin was proud of the people he accepted into his colony. He later wrote of them: "[They were] as good men as can be found in any part of the United States, and certainly more so than ever settled a frontier."

The success of Stephen Austin's colonial efforts encouraged others to come to Texas to receive grants as empresarios. Nearly all of those who applied for empresarioships were Americans. One exception was Lorenzo de Zavala of Mexico. By 1832, some 20 large grants, similar to Austin's, had been handed out. Some of the empresarios, who were unable to attract colonists to the remotest corners of the region, did not profit well. An 1837 map of Texas showed a total of 14,050 families living in Texas. Of that number, 11,300 lived on land that had been administered by Austin.

Austin did his best to serve his colonists well. He kept relations smooth between himself and the government in Mexico City. When American Indians killed some settlers, Austin formed a militia and drove them away. With other tribes, such as the Tonkawa and Wichita, he made treaties. He was receptive—perhaps overly so—to the complaints of his colonists. Still, he managed to keep the great majority satisfied with their new lives outside the United States.

Ironically, although Stephen Austin had originally opposed his father's plan to establish a colony in Texas, once he accepted the obligation to start the colony following his father's death, he spent the rest of his life serving those who purchased grant lands. Austin took on the role of empresario and never looked back. The job occupied all his energy and time. He never found the time to marry and never had children. Serving constantly as the go-between for the Mexican government and his colonists, he

An Early Revolt That Failed

Though some empresarios, such as Stephen Austin, tried hard to maintain consistent, positive relations with Mexico, other colonial leaders in Texas did not. One such leader was an empresario named Haden Edwards. In the fall of 1825, Edwards went to Texas with his brother, Benjamin, intent on establishing a colony. He convinced the Mexican government to grant him 300,000 acres (121,406 hectares) of land near the East Texas settlement of Nacogdoches. There, he said, he would settle 800 immigrant families. However, as Edwards claimed his land, he discovered that some settlers—both Americans and Mexicans— were already living on his property. Some of them had legitimate land titles that had been granted to them by the former Spanish government.

Angered by their presence, Edwards demanded that the settlers show him proof of their claims. He threatened to remove anyone who did not "show me their titles or documents." Feeling threatened, the settlers appealed to the Mexican government. In response, the president of Mexico allowed the earlier inhabitants to remain on their lands and revoked the Edwards brothers' grant. He even ordered Haden and Benjamin Edwards out of Texas. Armed with an order from the Mexican president, the earlier settlers began evicting the newer settlers from their lands.

When word of the order reached Texas in June 1826, Haden Edwards was on a trip to the United States. Benjamin Edwards did not intend to leave Texas without a fight. He began to rally his immigrant supporters, calling for a revolt against Mexican authority. In mid-December, Benjamin led a group of three dozen angry colonists in Nacogdoches. They carried a banner that read: "Independence, Liberty, and Justice." They occupied the local fort and announced the establishment of the Republic of Fredonia.

Then, everything began to fall apart. Benjamin Edwards expected help in his revolt from newly arrived Cherokee Indians, who were angry that the Mexican government would not grant them land. That support faded quickly, though. Then, in January 1827, a unit of 250 Mexican troops arrived, with 100 settlers from Austin's colony backing them up. By the time they arrived, the Fredonians had scattered. The Republic of Fredonia was no more.

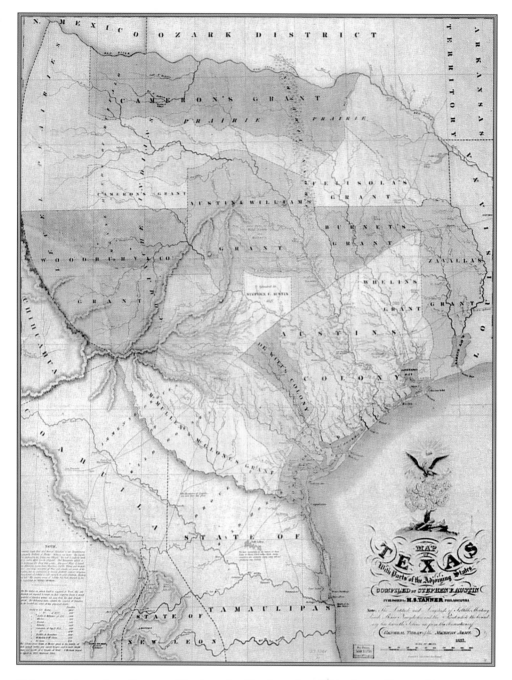

This map, based on the one Stephen Austin drew in 1837, shows the outline of each land grant in Texas. The list at the bottom left is a count of the people living in each colony.

wrote official letters to Mexico City and made trips to meet with government officials. Despite the vastness of his personal land holdings, Austin lived an unadorned life in a dog-trot cabin, a pair of cabins connected by a covered walkway. He enjoyed good conversations with friends, as well as the occasional frontier party, complete with dancing and fiddle music. He was often alone, however. Austin once described his daily existence as "coffee, corn-bread, milk and butter, and a bachelor's household, which is confusion, dirt, and torment."

With the favor of the Mexican government, with their colony situated on a land that was ripe for farming, and under the watchful eye of Stephen Austin, the American colonists prospered. By 1830, more than a dozen villages had sprung up, and some were even developing into towns, complete with "brick stores and frame dwelling houses." Austin's town of San Felipe was home to more than 200 colonists by 1828. Its residents lived in pleasant log cabins and could find the necessities of life in a pair of locally owned general stores. Nearly everyone farmed, relying primarily on corn production, which provided the basic ingredient for bread and alcohol, as well as food for livestock. Second to corn production was cotton cultivation. A significant number of whites who emigrated to Texas brought along their slaves to help tend the crops. By 1833, cotton production reached 4,000 bales, then 10,000 by 1834. That same year, in the district of the Brazos alone, colonists maintained 25,000 head of cattle.

The local economies of the American settlers were largely cashless. Instead of using money, the colonists bartered for what they needed. It was a lively exchange, not unlike the way they had done business in rural America: "clothing made in Europe traded for hogs, horses exchanged for corn, an ox for a sow, a feather bed for three cows with calves, a gun for a mare." When they traded their produce out to distant markets, they did not typically cart their goods south to San Antonio de Béxar, the closest Mexican community of size. In his book *Lone Star*, historian T. R. Fehrenbach described the dual relationships and loyalties that existed within the American settlements:

> The colony was subject, of course, to all the laws, rules, regulations . . . first of Spain, then of independent Mexico. But actually, the Anglo settlements lay completely outside Mexican Texas. They were planted on completely empty ground, hundreds of miles from the nearest historic town or fort. By their location, high up on the Texas coastal plain, they were removed from and outside the economic sphere of San Antonio de Béxar. Lack of money and the absence of good roads handicapped trade with San Antonio; the Anglo colonies looked back north, toward the United States.

This single factor—that the vast majority of the colonists who occupied Austin's land grants were Americans— would keep many of the newcomers focused not on developing loyalty to Mexico, but on fostering a continuing loyalty, even a longing, for the United States they had left behind.

Despite the advantages found in the rich, abundant Texas land, the immigrants to Mexican territory faced serious, long-term problems. They were living on the frontier. Since their land claims were so extensive, it was almost impossible to have close neighbors. Indian attacks were a constant threat. Travel was difficult, sometimes unthinkable, as roads were either nonexistent or, during rainy weather, impassable. With such distractions, some settlers must have longed to return to the United States, or at least wished for the United States's advantages on Texas soil.

Even so, those who came generally remained on their expansive Texas lands, and population and productivity continued to grow. During the first ten years of colonization, the population of the lands of the empresarios grew from 4,000 in 1821 to approximately 20,000 by 1830. By that date, the American population in Texas had far outstripped the indigenous Mexican population. Whole pockets of Texas were becoming, in many ways, Americanized. Despite these facts, few realized how much this continuing loyalty to the United States would set the course of events for Texas history during the next decade.

Samuel Houston, although not present at the siege of the Alamo, was the Texans' leading general. In fact, Houston ordered Jim Bowie to abandon the Alamo, but Bowie defied his orders.

A Land of Revolution

By 1830, the number of Americans who had migrated to Texas during the previous decade had begun to alarm the Mexican government in Mexico City. Throughout the 1820s, Mexican leaders and concerned aristocrats had watched the cultural climate of Texas shift away from Spanish–Mexican traditions. The Americans outnumbered Mexicans in Texas by ten to one. With the uneven balance came cultural changes. Americans had introduced a highly competitive economic and trade system. They brought more than 1,000 black slaves to the region. They did not even pretend to take Catholicism seriously. Americans educated their children in their own schools, or sent them back to the United States for their schooling. The Americans were not becoming more attuned to Hispanic culture; they continued to keep it at arm's length. When a Mexican general toured the region during 1828–1829, he reported his concerns to the government in Mexico City. It was suggested that the government of Mexico should develop a policy that would try to get many ethnic Mexicans to emigrate to Texas as soon as possible. The idea went nowhere, even though Mexican anxiety was quickly developing into fear.

At the same time, a feeling of restlessness and uneasiness may have been descending on the Americans who lived in the various Texas colonies. Stephen Austin felt it. By his second decade of serving the American immigrants across his broad colony, he was getting tired and cranky, and was feeling dejected. In his mind, his colonists were underappreciative of his efforts. He had poured himself into his empresarial role, and had juggled conflicting forces. His fellow empresarios had allowed a rougher class of people into their colonies, the kind of people Austin typically referred to as "leatherstockings." These were the frontiersmen of the American South and West. They were uncouth, uneducated, feisty, and ferociously independent. Trying to control them was out of the question. Still, the Mexican government decided on a course of action to meet the threat of these and other Americans in Texas.

In the spring of 1830, the Mexican Congress passed the Decree of April 6. One part of the new law, Article 11, declared that Texas was closed to any further colonization by Americans. In addition, all new imports of slaves were banned. To stem the tide of trade between the Texas colonists and markets in the United States, Mexican officials established customs duties and a collection process. No such duties had been placed on the Americans when they first entered Texas. The colonists did not accept these new restrictions willingly.

To the Mexicans, the duties and obligations placed on the Americans did not appear to be much of a burden. As the Mexican government attempted to change its relationship with its American colonists, however, the changes caused a considerable stir. At the heart of the problem was the fact that, prior to 1830, the Mexicans had neither held the Americans to any real obligations, nor had they felt the need to provide basic services to the colonists. In other words, the Americans did not pay, and the Mexican government did not provide. T.R. Fehrenbach described the earlier relationship of the 1820s colonial period:

> While Mexicans were subject to military service, taxes, customs duties, and mandatory church tithes, Anglo–Texans were not. Their government was left to the empresarios, who let them regulate themselves . . . [In exchange,] the colonists were given no military protection or government services of any kind. The Anglo–Texans were simply allotted lands the Mexicans had never been able to use, and within ten years they were chipping out a . . . commonwealth rich in natural resources, where every man with a white skin was more or less equal with his league of land, and hampered by no distant government, beneficial or otherwise.

Suddenly, the Mexican government, under the leadership of President Anastacio Bustamante, was ready to begin acting like something it had never been to the Americans— a government.

The Americans believed they now faced a serious threat from the Mexican government that had largely ignored them for ten years. Little changed immediately, however.

Then, in 1831, the Mexican military, under the command of Don Manuel de Mier y Terán, a Mexican official who hated Americans, began to place troop garrisons across Texas to enforce the laws passed the previous year. Three hundred fifty Mexican troops were stationed in the town of Nacogdoches. Hundreds more patrolled the Gulf Coast, in search of American smugglers who were attempting to avoid paying customs duties. More troops were sent to La Bahia and San Antonio.

The Texans' response was immediate. They held protest meetings and committed occasional acts of violence. Philosophically, the Texans believed that Mexico had no right to change its course and policies after a decade of neglect. Texans argued they had been granted self-government by the 1824 Mexican Constitution. Suddenly, every old assumption seemed to be falling aside.

Then, in late December 1831, trouble erupted. When the Mexican state government in Coahuila installed a new governor, he ignored parts of the Decree of 1830 and allowed additional Americans to make land claims. When he did so, General Mier y Terán responded angrily. He ordered the arrest of the Texas land officials who had granted the titles to the new American arrivals. One of the general's officers, Captain John Bradburn, entered the town of Liberty, declared the community nonexistent, and took control of the land grants. In addition, Bradburn went beyond his initial orders and closed all but one of the Texans' ports. His arrogance in dealing with both Americans and Mexicans in the region made nearly everyone angry. Bradburn was already despised by many Americans. He was not an ethnic Mexican, but an American, born in Kentucky, who worked as a Mexican official. The hated Mexican American remained on the scene through the spring of 1832. He drew more criticism from the Texans when, in May, he placed a large section of American colonial property under military rule and arrested several Americans, including a young lawyer from Alabama named William B. Travis. Travis's name was already fairly well known across parts of Texas, although he had arrived in the region just a year earlier. William Travis was destined to become one of the best-remembered names of the then-developing Texas Revolution.

William Travis was born in 1809 in South Carolina, but his family moved to Alabama when he was just a boy. As a young man, he studied law, working as a teacher to pay his way through school. When he was 19, he married one of his students, the daughter of a wealthy planter. Three years later, the couple divorced, after Travis accused his young bride of adultery. With his life in disarray, the young Travis headed west in search of a more promising future.

In a few months, he arrived in Texas and staked a land claim. After a brief stay on the Gulf Coast, he moved to San Felipe, where he practiced law. There, he helped settlers file papers and write wills. He took one case on behalf of a man who had purchased a blind horse. He accepted any payment a client could afford. Once, he took a pair of oxen as a fee.

Travis lived in a boardinghouse, liked to gamble, and had a string of affairs with a number of local women. People in San Felipe knew him for his flamboyant clothing. He often wore a white hat with the broadest brim imaginable, the kind typical of Southern plantation owners, and red pants. Travis was a complicated man. Despite his taste for partying and constant women, he was known as a gentleman. Perhaps surprisingly, he was also known as a highly religious man. Travis was ambitious, well read, self-focused, "moody, touchy, [and was] easily offended." But he was also a man of action and principle.

William Travis, who came to Texas after a divorce, was a complicated man. Although he was very religious, he also loved to gamble and go to parties.

By 1831–1832, Colonel Bradburn was clamping down on men such as Travis and his fellow Texans. One day, Travis and a friend told Bradburn that 100 armed Texans were approaching Anahuac in Galveston Bay. The Mexican–American official prepared for the attack, keeping himself and his men awake throughout the night. When Bradburn realized he had been tricked by Travis's joke, Travis and his friend were arrested and nearly executed.

Even after Travis's release, Bradburn remained a symbol of Mexican tyranny in Texas. During 1832, Travis became convinced that the Mexican government and the Texan Americans were on a course that would result in an eventual clash of arms. That year, he joined a local "War Party," a group of Texans bent on pursuing the independence of Texas from Mexico.

In the summer of 1832, nearly 100 Texas colonists, led by John Austin, marched on the coastal town of Liberty in an uprising against Bradburn. There, some Texans met with Colonel José de las Piedras, whose small contingent of men was greatly outnumbered by the furious residents. During the meeting, Piedras promised to have Bradburn removed from his seat of authority. When Bradburn received the news, he angrily resigned his post.

Meanwhile, Austin and his followers, who had not been part of the Piedras negotiations, remained in the field, desperately searching for cannons. In time, they armed a schooner with three cannons, then sailed down the Brazos River toward Anahuac. Their advance was halted by the presidio at Velasco. When Mexican authorities refused to stand down, John Austin's men opened fire on the fort. With the cannons blasting away, several dozen Texan marksmen took positions on the schooner's deck, protected by cotton bales. As Mexican cannoneers attempted to fire the fort's cannon, the Texas riflemen picked them off one by one. Before the fight was over, the Mexican garrison had lost many of its men.

Later that summer, on August 2–3, another violent clash took place between Texans and Mexican authorities, this time at Nacogdoches. After a Mexican commandant ordered residents to turn in all their firearms, local colonists, led by a brash Louisianian named Jim Bowie, attacked the Mexican garrison and took everyone, including the commandant, prisoner. Bowie and his men ordered the Mexican troops to swear their loyalty to the reform-minded General Antonio López de Santa Anna. At the time, the Texas revolutionaries were rallying in the name of Santa Anna, the general who had declared himself to be the liberal voice of Mexico and claimed to be ready to bring down the tyranny of the Mexican government.

With these early victories, much of the shooting of the Texas Revolution had taken place. Most importantly, though, the Texan successes at Velasco and Anahuac meant that the last of the Mexican soldiers garrisoned on Texas soil were removed.

As political and cultural clashes led to violence, the original American empresario, Stephen Austin, was desperately searching for ways to bridge the widening gulf between the Mexican government and the Americans in Texas. He had always tried to maintain good relations with Mexico, and he had taken care of several problems during more than a decade of colonization. In 1833, he still saw himself as a loyal citizen of Mexico. Austin had always believed that the Mexican government would eventually allow Texas to become a separate Mexican state. Mexican officials had promised this from the beginning. Austin decided to take a trip to Mexico City in the summer of 1833, thinking the time was right to apply for state status for Texas. A new constitution had been written, which he carried to the Mexican capital. In Austin's mind, given the deterioration of relations between Mexico and Americans in Texas, it was now or never. Once there, Austin campaigned for Texas recognition as a full-fledged Mexican state. He complained about the neglect Texas had endured at the hands of the Mexican government. He noted that there was not a single civil court in Texas. He argued that "Texas needs a government, and that the best she can have, is to be created a State in the Mexican Federation."

Austin soon found himself unwelcome in Mexico City, and his petition for Texas statehood was looked upon with suspicion. Earlier that year, Santa Anna had been elected president of Mexico. The popular Santa Anna had not intended to hold office, but instead planned to pass the government on to his vice president, a reformer named Valentín Gómez Farías. However, Santa Anna removed Farías from power through a military takeover. Soon, Santa Anna became reactionary, refusing to enact reforms, while he extended harsh control over Texas.

The years from 1833 to 1834 proved decisive for the developing Texas Revolution. Austin left Mexico City uncertain about the future, but still clinging to the possibility of eventual state status for his beloved Texas, even though Santa Anna's government had denied the request. Before he arrived back in Texas, however, agents of Santa Anna arrested Austin and returned him to Mexico City, where he was imprisoned. He was accused of having delivered a letter to the council in San Antonio that instructed them to continue to push for Texas statehood. Because his letter was a direct violation of the decision that had been made in Mexico City in regard to statehood, Santa Anna was prepared to come down hard on the longtime loyal empresario. Austin's imprisonment only removed his moderate voice from the events taking place in Texas for the rest of 1834. He was released in December of that year.

When Austin proved unable to provide direction for his fellow Texans, another leader stepped forward—a former governor of the state of Tennessee, Sam Houston. Houston had only arrived on the Texas scene the previous year, but his name was already known. He had lived as a young man among the Cherokee Indians of Tennessee, who had adopted him. During the War of 1812, Houston served as a 20-year-old infantry lieutenant under General Andrew Jackson, who was also from Tennessee. During one battle with Creek Indians, young Houston had received two musket ball wounds to the shoulder. After the war, he worked as an agent to the Cherokee, whom he served well. Over the following years, Houston studied law and passed the bar examination. Making a name for himself across Tennessee, Houston was elected to be the state's attorney general in 1819. By 1823, at the age of 30, he was elected as a member of the U.S. House of Representatives.

Within another four years, Houston was elected governor of Tennessee. In 1829, he married Eliza Allen, a shy and quiet young girl. The marriage would prove disastrous. After only three months, his bride, 15 years younger than her husband, returned to her parents. Neither Houston nor his wife ever gave an explanation for their separation and subsequent divorce. Some blamed Houston's drinking; others suspected that Eliza was still in love with another man, one her parents had bypassed in favor of the flamboyant governor of Tennessee. As public speculation grew, Houston expressed his feelings: "This is a painful, but it is a private affair. I do not recognize the right of the public to interfere."

Humiliated by the turn of events, Houston resigned the governorship and dropped out of the Tennessee spot-light. He decided to live with the Cherokee. Andrew Jackson, now U.S. president, had ordered the Cherokee to leave their ancestral lands and move west of the Mississippi River. Houston went west to join them. On his way across the Arkansas Territory, Houston experienced a strange event that seemed to indicate to him that he was heading in the right direction for his own future.

He recalled: "An eagle swooped down near my head, and then, soaring aloft with wildest screams, was lost in the rays of the settling sun. I knew that a great destiny waited for me in the West." Houston's "great destiny" would have to wait, however. Over the next three years, living among his adopted people, Houston spent much of his time drinking or drunk. The American Indians he lived with noticed this and began to call him "Oo-tse-tee Ar-dee-tah-skee," which meant "Big Drunk."

By 1832, Houston came to a personal crossroads and became determined to turn his life around. For years, he had talked about Texas. Now, amid the swirl of rumors and stories of the anti-Mexican rebellion sweeping across Texas, Houston decided to be a part of the future of Texas.

When he arrived in Nacogdoches, then the largest American settlement in the Texas colonies, he immediately made some new friends and met some old ones, including Jim Bowie, whom Houston had met on a steamboat three years earlier. Bowie, famous throughout the Southwest, had arrived in Texas four years earlier. Born in Louisiana and raised in Mississippi bayou country, Bowie was a colorful figure. As a teenager, he was known to have wrestled alligators. When he was in his twenties and thirties, he became a slave smuggler and land speculator. In Texas, Bowie was recognized as someone who ran in both American and Mexican circles. After his arrival, he had married a young Mexican woman, the daughter of one of the wealthy landed families of the region.

Houston spent his first Christmas in Texas with Bowie, who introduced the newly arrived Tennesseean to several prominent Mexican leaders. Houston also met Stephen Austin. After their meeting, which lasted several hours, Austin, who was losing control over events in Texas, realized that men such as Houston would probably determine the future of the Americanized region. Austin wrote about the differences between himself and Houston:

> A successful military chieftain is hailed with admiration and applause and monuments perpetuate his fame. But the bloodless pioneer of the wilderness, like the corn and cotton he causes to spring where it never grew before, attracts no notice. No slaughtered thousands or smoking cities attest his devotion to the cause of human happiness, and he is regarded by the mass of the world as a humble instrument to pave the way for others.

Houston was, as Austin believed, destined to play an important role in the approaching history of Texas. The region soon became the source of his new identity, the place of his public rebirth. Only weeks after his arrival, Houston came to believe that Texas should be independent of Mexican control.

During 1834, Austin's eclipse was becoming certain, while Houston's star was definitely rising. Austin's moderate influence drew less support as President Santa Anna grew increasingly tyrannical. Early revolutionary clashes in Texas had focused on reforming the relationship between the prairie colonies and Mexico. Now reform was giving way to radicalism. By 1835, the Mexican general-dictator had created a puppet government in Mexico and dissolved the state legislature. He denied the request for Mexican statehood for Texas, dispatched an army to the region to direct the collection of customs duties, and ordered the Texas militia to be reduced in number to no more than one militiaman for every 500 residents.

From the beginning, the Texans had refused to abide by the customs laws placed on them by Mexico. They

Jim Bowie was a controversial figure who had been known as a smuggler and speculator. He also took part in several skirmishes with American Indians, which gave him military experience that would be valuable during the Texas Revolution.

continued to trade, even illegally, with other Americans, who could provide manufactured goods through U.S. trading communities such as St. Louis and New Orleans. By 1834, the value of the goods being smuggled between the United States and Texas amounted to more than 200,000 pesos (Mexican currency) annually. When Santa

A Frontier Weapon of Legend

Although Jim Bowie's name will always remain linked to the events of the Texas Revolution and especially the siege at the Alamo, the Bowie name has another legacy. A legendary frontier weapon still bears his name: the Bowie knife. During the first half of the nineteenth century, many western Americans carried weapons for protection and other uses. The handguns of the period were awkward, wildly inaccurate, and often expensive. Most of those who carried a weapon chose a knife. A favorite model was invented by Jim Bowie. Because of its size and deadly capabilities, the Bowie knife won a reputation of its own.

The Bowie knife was an extraordinarily versatile weapon. As one writer explained, it could "stab like a dagger, slice like a razor and chop like a cleaver." Models varied, but a typical Bowie knife might feature a blade of 9-to-15 inches in length that was sharpened on one side to the blade's curve, and on both sides to the knife's point. Most models included a brass handguard that allowed its wielder to use it in several ways without the risk of personal injury. Most had wooden handles of either walnut or hickory, but some sported antler or bone handles. The average Bowie knife might weigh as much as a pound (half a kilogram).

This knife's unique design made it a weapon designed for killing, not for hunting. Jim Bowie certainly put his to use more than once, causing the death of an opponent. Bowie first used an early model—one that was more like a butcher knife than the later design—in 1827 when he served as a second during a duel. After the duel broke out into a brawl, Bowie used his knife to slash two men to death. He used his Bowie knife again in 1830, when he was ambushed by three would-be killers in Texas. Bowie struck down all three with his knife, slicing the throat of one, the stomach of the second, and delivering a fatal head wound to the third. Such actions helped create Bowie's legacy as a rough-and-tumble frontiersman.

Bowie did not kill every time he used his knife, however. During an 1832 stagecoach ride, Bowie drew his knife and threatened the life of a fellow passenger after he refused to put out his pipe at the request of a female rider. Onboard the stagecoach was a fourth passenger, the famous U.S. politician Henry Clay, who witnessed the incident, unaware of Jim Bowie's reputation. Afterwards, whenever Clay retold the story, he would speak of Jim Bowie as "the greatest fighter in the Southwest."

Anna reopened the Customs House at Anahuac in 1835, he sent an army officer, Captain Antonio Tenorio, to direct the collections. The Mexican general was prepared to crack down severely on smugglers. After Tenorio's men seized a Texas schooner, *Martha*, with supplies bound for the American colonists, William Travis organized several dozen men, and the group forced Tenorio and his men to leave Anahuac. During the late June standoff, Travis had warned Tenorio to surrender or be "put to the sword." After a single cannon shot, the 45-man Mexican force had surrendered.

When word of Travis's armed insurrection reached Santa Anna, he was furious. He resolved, once and for all, to end Texas hostility and force the Americans to accept his authority. He intended to teach the Texans a lesson. In short order, he dispatched his brother-in-law, General Martín Perfecto de Cos, to Texas, with orders to arrest Travis and any other Texans who were bent on defying Mexican authority.

General Antonio López de Santa Anna was both the presidential dictator of Mexico and the military leader who moved his forces to put down the Texas Revolution.

The Texans Defend Themselves

Despite the stirring nature of the Travis raid on Anahuac and the assault on Tenorio, many Texans, even in 1835, still opposed a revolution to try to free Texas from Mexican authority. For that reason, many Americans in Texas harshly criticized Travis for his actions. The pendulum was about to swing in the opposite direction, however. Once Santa Anna sent a Mexican army northward to bring the Texans back in line, many of those who had opposed Texas separation turned against the Mexican leader. Before the recent clashes with the Mexican authorities, the Texans believed they were only seeking fairness and control of their local destiny as a recognized Mexican state. With the arrival of General Cos's army, though, the Americans became ready to defend themselves, their homes, and their future.

Soon, broadsides were published, calling for Texas independence from Mexican tyranny. Santa Anna became the object of almost universal scorn and hatred across the Texas prairies. Samuel Houston spoke to crowds of Texans as large as 1,000 and rallied them in preparation for the Mexican showdown that seemed to be coming. He sent a letter to a Louisiana newspaper, the *Red River Herald*, with a desperate request: "Let each man come with a good rifle and 100 rounds of ammunition—and come soon." William Travis wrote with patriotic fervor about the honor and destiny of Texas. Jim Bowie rode south with his men to scout out Mexican movements, only to report back that a Mexican army was landing at the small settlement of Matamoros, on the banks of the Rio Grande river.

As Cos's army marched toward San Antonio, the Texans gathered together in a convention on October 15, 1835. They had already held a council with Stephen Austin, who had returned on September 1 from a two-year absence in Mexico. Austin had always been the voice of restraint, but after his imprisonment in Mexico City, he was a changed man. With Texas on the verge of war with Mexico, Austin assured the revolutionary leaders that negotiating with Santa Anna was impossible. He described the general as a "base, unprincipled bloody monster." No longer holding his ground in favor of loyalty to the Mexican government, Austin assured the Texans: "War is our only recourse. We must defend our rights, ourselves and our country, by force of arms."

Men soon rallied by the thousands to defend their homeland. Fortunately, many of them had already completed their fall harvest, which allowed them to leave their farms without much disruption.

Just days before the meeting at Washington-on-the-Brazos, Cos had already arrived in San Antonio de Béxar and taken up defensive positions inside the abandoned mission church of San Antonio de Valero. In recent years, the old church had been used more than once to garrison Spanish or Mexican troops. Once, it had housed a Spanish colonial company from Alamo de Parras, Mexico. Over the years, the old mission had come to be called the "Alamo."

The Texans who marched fervently toward San Antonio did not wear regular uniforms, since they were not part of a regular army. They were strictly a volunteer force, providing their own rifles and lead. Discipline did not come easy and during the march toward San Antonio, approximately 150 members of Austin's 500-man force left their unit to make a side trip home to retrieve warm clothes. One member of the Texas force described his comrades:

> Buckskin breeches were the nearest approach to uniform and there was a wide diversity even there. . . . Boots being an unknown quantity, some wore shoes and some moccasins. Here a broad-brimmed sombrero overshadowed the military cap at its side . . . Here a big American horse loomed up above the nimble Spanish pony . . . there a half-broke mustang pranced beside a sober, methodical mule . . . in lieu of a canteen each man carried a Spanish gourd . . . A fantastic military array to a casual observer, but the one great purpose animating every heart clothed us in a uniform more perfect in our eyes than was ever donned by regulars on dress parade.

By late October, the force of Texans advancing on San Antonio had sent out a scouting mission. Led by Jim Bowie, the 90-man advance unit ran into a contingent of 400 Mexican dragoons. A fight broke out, as the Mexicans

produced several cannons that they prepared to fire on
Bowie and his men. As the Texans poured withering rifle
fire against the Mexican troops, the enemy abandoned the
field, leaving its cannons behind. As the Texans turned the
Mexican artillery around, the battle ended with the loss of

The Sad Tale of the "Come and Take It" Cannon

While Cos and his forces marched on San Antonio, the Mexican commandant in Béxar, Colonel Domingo de Ugartechea, sent a unit of Mexican troops east to the settlement of Gonzales to retrieve a small brass cannon that he heard had fallen into the hands of the Texans. Artillery was in short supply, and each available field piece was highly prized by both armies. For a while, a group of Texans had buried the cannon in question in a peach orchard and plowed over it to keep it safe. When the word went out of the Mexican troops' move on Gonzales, Texans flocked by the dozens to the small village, prepared to defend it and its valuable artillery piece against an advance of 100 Mexican cavalrymen. When the Mexicans arrived, nearly 200 Texans had gathered at Gonzales, armed with their long rifles. The cannon had been placed on an ox cart on which a sign was hung. The sign read: "Come and Take It."

The cannon was not, in reality, a very important piece of artillery. It was small and stubby, measuring less than three feet in length and weighing about 70 pounds. It had been in Texas for nearly 25 years, brought in by a group of Americans who hoped to wrest Texas from Mexico. The cannon had been seized by Spanish soldiers. By the time of the Texas Revolution, the sorry old artillery piece was on its last legs. Still, to the Texans of Gonzales, it was worth fighting for.

On the morning of October 2, the Texans and the Mexican dragoons engaged in a brief skirmish. A Texas artilleryman named Almaron Dickinson used the cannon to fire a barrage of old horseshoes and nails at the Mexicans, since cannonballs were nearly as scarce as cannons themselves. In a short time, the Mexican forces, outnumbered and outgunned, abandoned

60 Mexican soldiers. Only one Texan died.

As the main party of Austin's Texans, the "Army of the People," approached San Antonio de Béxar, General Cos was soon surrounded. By November 1, the noose was tight around him. Once the Texans had Cos trapped in Béxar,

the fight. They made their way back to San Antonio to report to their commander. One Mexican soldier had been killed in the fight.

The Gonzales victory was followed a week later by the Texans' capture of the settlement at Goliad, located 90 miles southeast of San Antonio de Béxar. There, the Texans forced the surrender of a unit of Mexican soldiers who had taken up a position in an old mission building. General Cos had sent them there to establish rear protection for his supply lines. The victory allowed the Texans to capture two cannons and hundreds of muskets.

The story of the prized "Come and Take It" cannon did not end there, however. After the fight for the cannon, a force of 500 Texas men began to march from Gonzales toward General Cos's army. Among the Texans was Jim Bowie. The troops were led by the moderate-turned-revolutionary Stephen Austin, then in his early forties. The army of revolutionaries carried the small, six-pound (2.7-kilogram) cannon they had defended at Gonzales on a makeshift cart—really nothing more than two pieces of tree trunk slapped together—pulled by longhorn steers. The men carried a makeshift flag, a white banner featuring a single black star, a cannon barrel, and the words: "Come and Take It." The emblem would become known as the Old Cannon Flag.

A twist of events rendered the precious cannon useless to the advancing Texans. Texas roads of the time were extremely poor. The friction and grinding caused the cart's wheels and axles to screech and smoke. After the Texans had covered half the distance between Gonzales and San Antonio, the wheels fell off the cart, and the cannon the Texans had once defended so bravely had to be abandoned and buried once again, this time at a place called Sandy Creek.

however, they were uncertain of their next move. Despite their growing numbers, they still faced 1,400 Mexican troops who had taken up defensive positions in the small Texas settlement. Austin began to lose control of his men. Sam Houston appeared on the scene briefly, having arrived from San Felipe, where the General Consultation had been established to iron out the details of the provisional government of Texas. Austin tried to pass command of his volunteer units to Houston, but Houston had not come to San Antonio to fight. Instead, he had come to round up delegates for the consultation, which had not been able to meet because it lacked a quorum. When Houston left, he took several Texans with him.

The men who gathered at the consultation on November 3, 1835, did not vote in favor of Texas independence. Instead, they promised to support the Mexican Constitution of 1824, under which they had been allowed to migrate to Texas in the first place. The delegates did vote, however, to move toward independence if the Mexican government failed to recognize the validity of the Constitution of 1824. The consultation then elected a provisional government, including a governor. To organize the defense of Texas, Sam Houston was voted in as the commander of the Texas army. Austin was chosen as an official agent who would try to muster support from the United States for the beleaguered Texans. Although Jim Bowie attended the meeting, according to one eyewitness, he spent most of the sessions drunk. (Bowie had faced personal tragedy in 1833 when his wife and children all succumbed to cholera, a loss from which he never recovered emotionally.)

With Texans ringing the frontier settlement of San Antonio de Béxar, a siege developed, with Cos and his Mexican forces locked into a defensive posture. Throughout the first weeks of November, there was hardly any action.

Without adequate artillery, there was little the Texans could do to force Cos from his position. A direct assault on the Mexican town was seen as suicide. Order broke down within the ranks of the Texans, and some volunteers, who had signed on for only two months' service, abandoned the fight. With Austin assigned to drum up support for the Texas revolt, command of the besieging army fell to Colonel Edward Burleson.

A brief skirmish did occur on November 26, when several Mexican troops emerged from Béxar to collect hay to feed their livestock. During the short battle, which was called the "grass fight," the Texans killed about 50 of the enemy. Beyond that, there was little military action.

In the tedium of the siege, one Texas volunteer killed another, and the murderer was hanged from a pecan tree. By December, though, most of the Texas militia had abandoned the siege. They were tired of the inactivity and their enlistments were completed.

Then, suddenly, on December 2, two Americans who lived in San Antonio, Sam Maverick and John W. Smith, managed to slip out of the village to meet with their fellow Texans. The escapees brought maps of Cos's positions. They also reported what was happening in Béxar, that Cos's army was starving and running low on ammunition. The two men tried to convince Burleson that the time was right for an assault on Béxar.

For the next two days, Burleson debated whether to attack San Antonio. The colonel's officers wanted to call off the siege. On December 4, the order was given to abandon Béxar and retreat to Gonzales.

Many of the Texans were not happy with the decision. When Burleson seemed to be surrendering San Antonio without a fight, one Texan named Ben Milam took charge and offered to lead the assault. Milam, a 47-year-old Welsh-man from Kentucky, had lived in Texas even before Stephen

Austin's colony was founded. He had once spent time in a Mexican jail for supporting the idea of a republican government for Texas. He spoke to his fellows in arms: "Boys, who will come with old Ben Milam into San Antonio?" Immediately, several hundred men got ready for an assault. "Then fall in line!" shouted Milam.

The next day, December 5, at 3:00 A.M., the assault on General Cos's position in San Antonio began. Approximately 300 Texans were divided into two columns, one under the command of Milam. Over the next four days, the Texas volunteers fought their way through the streets of Béxar. Cos had divided his men into two units. One was situated in the small community of houses, shops, and other buildings, while the second held positions within the walls of the Alamo mission compound. Each half of Cos's forces had artillery at its disposal.

Milam's men broke through Cos's picket lines and then drove their way into San Antonio, fighting house to house. Much of the action was close in and hand-to-hand. The Texas riflemen were deadly as they picked off the enemy one by one. Historian T. R. Fehrenbach described the desperate, often chaotic street fighting:

> On the third day of this bitter . . . fighting, old Ben Milam . . . exposing himself and leading the bloody advance from house to house, was shot dead. . . . The assault went on. Some houses were reduced room by room. Battering rams, made of logs brought in from the sawmill, knocked down doors, and rifle butts smashed in Mexican faces. The Mexicans responded with heavy cannonades, which knocked down walls but killed few Texans.

On December 8, Cos was reinforced by 600 men who had arrived from south of Béxar. Throughout the entire

Ben Milam, a 47-year-old Welshman from Kentucky, rallied 300 Texans and stormed General Cos' army barricaded in San Antonio on December 5, 1835. Although Milam was killed by a Mexican sniper during the attack, Cos surrendered four days later.

battle, the Mexicans outnumbered the Texans by three to one. The fighting was not to the liking of the Mexican forces. They were trained to fight across open territory, on battlefields where they could maneuver and use cannons effectively against the enemy. Street fighting only suited the Texans. It was a style of fighting that represented a brawl as much as a military engagement. By December 9, Cos had had enough. Almost 200 of the Mexican forces situated around the Alamo grounds abandoned the fight and fled. Those who remained faced the onslaught of cannons at the hands of the furious Texans.

After Cos ordered a rider to deliver a white flag to the Texans, Burleson rode into the town and accepted the general's surrender. Cos delivered 1,100 of his men to Burleson. The Texas commander showed mercy to the captives, ordering all of them first to pledge that they would not fight the Texans again. He also made them promise to uphold the Constitution of 1824. Then, after the troops were supplied with enough powder and lead to protect themselves against possible Indian assault, Cos's army was sent away in the direction of Mexico City.

For many of the Texas revolutionary fighters, the victory at San Antonio de Béxar and at the Alamo mission signaled the end of Mexican military tyranny in Texas. With the defeat of General Cos, the Mexican government could not refuse to accept the Texans' wishes to abide by the Constitution of 1824 and become an independent Mexican state. Burleson disbanded his army and relieved himself of command. Many of his men began to return to their homes.

The fighting was not over, however. Nor had Mexico's resolve to destroy the revolutionary movement in Texas been weakened. General Cos returned to Mexico City to tell the story of how he had faced defeat with honor and had vowed never to fight the Texans again. His brother-in-law would hear none of it. From his palace in the capital of Mexico, Antonio López de Santa Anna, himself a general as well as the presidential dictator of Mexico, strapped on a $7,000 sword. He ordered his men, including the troops of General Cos, to march on Texas and defeat the revolutionary movement once and for all. Santa Anna was not yet ready to surrender Mexico's interest in the lands north of the Rio Grande.

An extremely vain man, General Santa Anna had a fondness for elaborately decorated uniforms.

The Siege Begins

For a time following the Mexican defeat at San Antonio, the Texas revolutionaries were without an enemy and without direction. As Cos and his troops marched out of Texas, the Texans were uncertain of their next move. Though many intended to abide by the revolution's original ideal of upholding the Mexican Constitution of 1824, that document had been voted out of existence by the Mexican legislature on Santa Anna's orders. By early 1836, under a new set of circumstances, it appeared that the revolutionaries needed to regear their revolt and consider a fight for complete independence from Mexican authority. The government of Texas was having trouble even gaining a quorum for its meetings, however. That meant that whatever might happen next would not be determined by politicians in Texas, but by a general in Mexico City.

When Santa Anna received word of the defeat of his brother-in-law, Cos, he was outraged. With little forethought or planning, Santa Anna began a march into Texas, with himself in command. San Antonio may have been lost for the moment. Even so, Santa Anna believed, it must not remain in Texan hands.

Even before the loss at Béxar, Santa Anna had spent millions building up his military. In just the year 1835, he virtually used up the entire Mexican treasury—a whopping $7.5 million—beefing up his army. In just weeks after the Mexican defeat at San Antonio, Santa Anna had collected an army of 6,000 men.

What kind of man was this Mexican general who was now intent on the destruction of all Texan resistance? He was a tall, handsome man, slender, with broad shoulders. He loved elaborate military uniforms. For Santa Anna, the more medals and gold braid, the better. (One of his uniforms was so heavy with silver that the metal was later melted down and cast into a set of spoons.) He also had a reputation with the ladies, and was known for his big ego. Although he was brave, he was also deathly afraid of water. For him, a river crossing was a nightmare, and on his march across Texas, he was forced to make several. As a military man, Santa Anna was a brilliant tactician and a man soldiers were willing to follow. He had won battles, including several against the Spanish during the Mexican war for independence less than 15 years earlier. Santa Anna was popularly known as the Napoleon of the West. In 1830, when he overthrew the Mexican president, Anastacio Bustamante, even the Texans had hailed Santa Anna as a hero. In time, though, Santa Anna revealed his true nature. He installed himself as a dictator and ordered the nullification of the Constitution of 1824. He was driven by a thirst

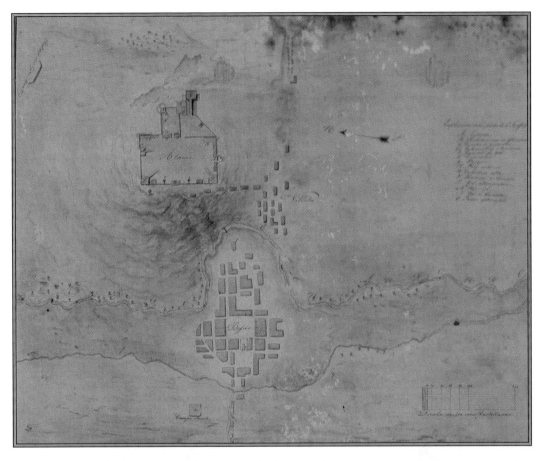

Santa Anna tried to keep his battle plan for the attack on the Alamo as simple as possible. This drawing was prepared by a Mexican army engineer to give a detailed view of the battlefield.

for power, as well as wealth and fame. He was remembered for having said on more than one occasion: "Man is nothing: power is everything!" and "Were I made God, I should wish to be something more." The egotistical Mexican general believed that his campaign would crush Texas resistance once and for all.

As Santa Anna formed his plan to meet the Texans in battle, he kept it simple. He would gather his men at Saltillo, north of Mexico City, then march northeast

Santa Anna's March Across Texas

As Santa Anna pushed his men across northern Mexico and into the province of Texas, members of his own army became the first casualties of his ego and poor planning. The army's progress was always painfully slow. In addition to his troops, Santa Anna's column included 1,800 pack mules carrying hardtack, a dried biscuit often eaten by armies of the day; 33 large four-wheeled wagons; 200 two-wheeled carts pulled by slowly plodding oxen; and hundreds of hangers-on who followed the army, selling the troops items, such as alcohol and tobacco, that were not provided by the Mexican army. The approaching army could be heard for miles, since the cart's gigantic seven-foot wooden wheels were unlubricated and made a loud screeching noise as the column advanced. Despite these problems, by February 12, the main Mexican army had reached the Rio Grande and met up with General Ramírez y Sesma.

With Sesma's troops added to Santa Anna's, the Mexican army that headed toward San Antonio numbered about 5,400. The soldiers also carried 21 cannons. The next day, however, the weather slowed the advance. On February 13, a blizzard nearly buried the army, which had no tents, leaving the soldiers and livestock to huddle together for warmth just to stay alive. Oxen wandered off in the face of the snowstorm, and many of the Mayan Indians who were counted among Santa Anna's troops froze to death. Grass for the livestock to eat was scarce, and the animals sometimes starved to death. Historian Walter Lord described Santa Anna's predicament:

> By now the men too were falling. Short of hardtack from the start, Santa Anna cut the troops to half-rations . . . forced them to shift for themselves on 12-and-a-half cents a day. Desperately, they took to the fields, chewing bitter mesquite nuts and munching reddish berries that looked possibly nourishing. Hundreds collapsed with dysentery and diarrhea. Others succumbed to a spotted itch. Still others dropped from sheer exhaustion. . . . The lack of doctors, drugs and ambulances . . . now proved fatal to scores of his men . . . it seemed a shame that Santa Anna had also forgotten to bring any chaplains.

Poor planning, bad weather, and the brutal ego of Santa Anna turned the Mexican march toward San Antonio into a hellish experience. These terrible circumstances led to a high rate of desertion among Santa Anna's men. Behind his advancing army, the Mexican general left a scattered trail of broken carts, worthless equipment, dead animals, and frozen men.

through Coahuila and along the El Camino Real, across Texas. The road would take him through San Antonio de Béxar, New Braunfels, Bastro, and Nacogdoches, and put him within striking distance of Gonzales, Goliad, and San Felipe de Austin. The march would require his army to cross nearly a dozen rivers, but the El Camino Real was the only route Santa Anna could follow that would bring his forces into the heart of Texas. Santa Anna himself reached Saltillo on January 7, 1836, where he fell violently ill for two weeks with a mysterious stomach ailment.

Santa Anna's strategy was so simple, it was even clear to the Texans. There was no main road besides the El Camino Real, and San Antonio would have to be the Mexican army's first and main objective. General Sam Houston certainly understood the strategy, but he refused to meet Santa Anna's army by holing up in the town of Béxar and defending the Alamo against a vastly larger army. Because the Texans would always be outnumbered in a fight, Houston understood that they needed mobility and flexibility on the field—something he would not have if he tried to hold on to the old mission grounds. By January 17, as the number of Texans still occupying San Antonio continued to dwindle through desertions, Houston sent out Jim Bowie and 30 other Texans with orders to destroy the mission. Houston also wrote to the provincial governor of Texas, Henry Smith, of his intentions: "I have ordered the fortifications in the town of Béxar to be demolished . . . And, if you should think well of it, I will remove all the cannon and other munitions of war to Gonzales and Copano, blow up the Alamo and abandon the place, as it will be impossible to keep up the Station with volunteers. . ."

After Bowie's departure for Béxar, Houston received a message from a Texan in San Antonio, who complained about the lack of pay for the men protecting Béxar as well as the lack of men. Despite the grievances it mentioned, the message was positive, even aggressive:

> Since we heard of 1000 to 1500 men of the enemy being on their march to this place duty is being shown well and punctually in case of an attack we will move all into the Alamo and whip 10 to 1 with our artillery. If the men here can get a reasonable supply of clothing, provisions and money they will remain the balance of the 4 months, and do duty and fight better than freshmen, they have all been tried and have confidence in themselves.

Although the people seemed ready to defend the Alamo, Bowie was already on his way to Béxar with orders to destroy the old Spanish mission. When he arrived, however, Bowie chose to follow his instincts, rather than Houston's orders. Bowie felt that the Alamo was too important a symbol to be destroyed. Bowie believed that it should be defended. As he made his rounds in San Antonio, he found the men there eager to defend the old mission. They had, after all, already beat the Mexicans once in Béxar's Alamo. A second round seemed certain to prove just as victorious. On January 26, a rally was held in San Antonio to call for the defense of the Alamo. A resolution was passed around for supporters to sign their names. Bowie was the second man to sign. With this decision, Bowie determined that the Alamo would be defended, and Houston's orders would be ignored.

Bowie explained his actions in a letter to Governor Smith, stating: "The salvation of Texas depends in great measure in keeping Béxar out of the hands of the enemy . . . if it were in the possession of Santa Anna, there is no stronghold from which to repel him in his march toward the Sabine [River in East Texas] . . . we will rather die in these ditches than give it up to the enemy."

Meanwhile, Santa Anna's march across northern Mexico continued. He and his men left Saltillo in late January, bound for the Rio Grande, where the general's forces would meet up with another Mexican army, under the command of General Joaquín Ramírez y Sesma. He had been sent the previous year to Texas to reinforce Cos in Béxar, but had not arrived before Cos's surrender. After the defeat, he had remained along the Rio Grande to wait for new orders.

Although the Texas men gathered in San Antonio de Béxar expected the arrival of Santa Anna's army, they did not think he would reach their position so early in the year. William Travis was certain that the Mexicans would wait until the spring grasses so they would have food for the horses and oxen. Thus, the Texans were not expecting Santa Anna until after mid-March. Even after Travis learned from a Mexican spy on February 20 that Santa Anna's forces had crossed the Rio Grande, he dismissed the report. It seemed too fantastic to believe. That very day, however, Santa Anna's advance troops were only 50 miles from Béxar.

Even though the Texans remained unconvinced that the approaching Mexican army was so near, they remained busy fortifying the old mission complex of the Alamo. The Texans knew a siege lay ahead. The problem was that the Alamo had not been built for defensive purposes. It had been a religious center, an eighteenth-century Catholic out-post built to convert local American Indians. The building and grounds, constructed about half a mile outside of San Antonio, on the opposite side of the San Antonio River, had been abandoned over 40 years earlier, and another church built in the town of Béxar itself. Since then, the Mexican army had used the old mission facilities as a barracks, but the grounds had remained in a semi-ruined condition. The center portion of the roof of the old mission church had long since collapsed. At its rear, or nave, an earthen ramp provided a rampart for a cannon emplacement. Some parts of the church were still intact. There, the rooms held a supply of gunpowder.

There were walls surrounding the perimeter of the mission grounds as well as a complex of buildings, including a two-story stone structure known as the Long Barracks and a one-story facility called the Low Barracks. The Long Barracks was located on the east side of the grounds, placing it at an angle, yet adjacent, to the church building. The Low Barracks was on the south side, closest to the San Antonio settlement that lay across the shallow river. The mission walls were made of mortar, two to three feet thick, and they stood between six and twelve feet high. The grounds enclosed by the walls measured approximately 250 by 450 feet. In front of the mission church, the walls came to an abrupt end, leaving a 75-foot-long gap that the mission defenders knew they would have to fill. Here, the Texans erected a low wall of sharpened stakes. Even so, when the battle began, this would remain the weakest point in the mission's defenses. The defenders reinforced the old walls, as well. The adobe on the north wall was falling apart, so the Texans built another crude wooden palisade to strengthen it. When the Mexican army arrived and the battle began, fewer than 200 men were inside the Alamo, defending nearly half a mile of perimeter walls.

At the center of the defensive efforts at the Alamo was a Texan named Green Jameson, a 29-year-old Texas lawyer who was a trained engineer. He directed the building of the palisade to fill the gap in front of the mission church, had parapets erected along the walls to provide placements for troops and cannon. Several artillery pieces were brought into the compound, including the garrison's prized cannon—an 18-pounder. This great iron cannon was the largest artillery weapon that could be found then in the entire region of

Texas. It was able to fire to a distance of half a mile a lead ball that usually weighed about 18 pounds (8 kilograms), which gave the cannon its name. Backing up this prized weapon, the Texans at the Alamo had about 20 other pieces of smaller artillery, including 12-pounders and 4-pounders. The Mexicans were only armed with light field cannons and howitzers, both short field guns. The amount of rifle and musket ammunition was good at the Alamo, but cannonballs were in short supply. This meant that the Texans sometimes were forced to fire their artillery with rusty door hinges, old nails, and other scraps of metal as ammunition.

During the weeks of January and February, as Santa Anna marched his men closer to their destiny at the Alamo, the number of Texan defenders grew, but only slightly. In mid-January, there were 114 men at the Alamo, with only 80 of them well enough for service, since sickness was a constant problem. When Jim Bowie and his men arrived, the number of defenders swelled to about 140. Not all of them were longtime residents of Texas. Many had only recently entered the northern Mexican province, ready to throw their lot in with the cause of independence. In fact, two out of every three men in the fortress were recent arrivals.

On February 8, the Texans received another welcome addition to their ranks. A unit of frontiersmen from the United States, calling themselves the Tennessee Mounted Volunteers, ambled into the streets of Béxar. Among them was a fighter everyone in the mission knew by name and reputation: Davy Crockett.

The 49-year-old Crockett was already a western legend. He had made a name as a frontiersman, living in log cabins and spending his days hunting. He claimed that he shot 47 bears in one month alone. Crockett had held public office in Tennessee and had recently served in the United States House of Representatives. He had published his autobiography, so the story of Davy Crockett was familiar to the men with whom he now sided inside the walls of the Alamo. Books and plays had been written about him—or at least about someone very similar to the folksy backwoodsman. Crockett had decided to make his way west to Texas after he lost his seat in Congress. After losing the election, he had announced to the people of Tennessee, "you may go to Hell, and I will go to Texas." He fulfilled his promise when he splashed across the waters of the Red River into Texas in early January. On January 9, he swore an oath to support the Texas Revolution: "I have taken the oath of government and have enrolled my name as a volunteer for six months." When Crockett arrived in Béxar, Jim Bowie rode out and met the outspoken Tennessean in a Mexican cemetery in drizzling rain. Crockett informed Bowie: "Me and my Tennessee boys, have come to Help Texas as privates and will try to do our duty." Crockett would prove a significant morale booster for the men as they prepared to engage the approaching Mexican army.

William Barret Travis became the commander of the garrison on February 11, after the previous commander, Colonel James Neill, passed authority to him. (Travis was the senior regular army officer in the compound, although he was 20 years younger than Neill.) Travis had arrived only a week earlier, though, and many of the volunteers did not want to follow his command. A number of men preferred to take orders from Jim Bowie. As a result, Travis and Bowie agreed to hold separate commands, but they also agreed to confer on major decisions. As the days progressed, Bowie proved to be of little help. He was often drunk, and then he became deathly ill. During nearly all the fighting that was to come, he was sick, unable even to get out of bed.

Although the report of Santa Anna's crossing of the Rio Grande on February 20 had been met with skepticism by the men at the Alamo, another report reached Travis the

Davy Crockett, frontiersman and politician, was already famous before he arrived in Texas and decided to join in the fight to defend the Alamo.

next day. Santa Anna's advance guard had arrived at the Medina River, just 25 miles outside San Antonio. That night, in fact, the Mexican leader planned to catch the Texans off-guard by sending a column of cavalry into San Antonio, but a sudden rainstorm brought the plan to a halt. By the following evening, Mexican advance forces could see the town from their positions in the hills to the south. On the morning of February 23, the residents of Béxar spotted the Mexican soldiers and began to flee the sleepy community in a panic. Travis, still in disbelief, sent two riders to investigate. They rode less than two miles toward the enemy positions before they returned to bring back the grim news: A column of Mexican dragoons was just beyond sight of the Alamo.

The bell in the church in San Antonio rang out, warning the Texans in Béxar to take refuge in the Alamo compound. Because he was so ill, Bowie had to be carried there. Some of the men brought their families with them into the fortress, including one of the artillery veterans, Almaron Dickinson, who rushed his 18-year-old wife, Susannah, and their 15-month-old baby inside the garrison. As the men left the town of San Antonio, they grabbed any food they could carry and brought the supplies to the Alamo.

Once the gates were closed, the Alamo siege began. One hundred fifty defenders were counted, ready for action. An additional 25 people were also in the compound, most of them women and children, as well as several black slaves, one of whom belonged to Travis. With the enemy close at hand, Travis knew that his inferior force would need reinforcements. While there was still time, Travis penned a note to be delivered to the Texas settlement at Gonzales, 70 miles to the east. His words revealed his desperate situation: "The enemy in large force is in sight. We want men and provisions. Send them to us. We have 150 men and are determined to defend the Alamo to the last. Give us assistance." Two riders were sent out of the compound around 3:00 P.M. on February 23. Meanwhile, a second message that was equally urgent was sent to the Texans at Goliad. Even as these hurried messengers whipped their horses to greater speeds, the Mexican cavalry was entering the streets of San Antonio.

All was confusion and anxious preparation as the men

inside the Alamo began to take positions. Davy Crockett approached Travis, telling him: "Colonel, here am I, assign me a position, and I and my Tennessee boys will defend it." (Whether Crockett actually said these words has been questioned by some historians.) Crockett had brought about a dozen men with him into the Alamo. The eager frontiersman was assigned to defend the most difficult portion of the perimeter walls: the 75-foot gap in front of the mission church. Other assignments were made and last-minute foragers made a mad dash outside the palisade walls for food, returning with 80 bushels of corn and nearly three dozen head of cattle. Food would not be a significant problem for the men inside the Alamo.

Across the river, in the now abandoned town of Béxar, the Texans spotted a red flag that the Mexicans had placed in the church bell tower. Everyone instantly knew its meaning. It was a symbolic message from Santa Anna that no prisoners would be taken during the fighting. He intended to crush the rebellion in Texas by destroying the men inside the old mission. Travis defiantly answered the flag message by order-ing the firing of the 18-pounder. Despite Travis's response, Jim Bowie sent a rider out under a white flag to see if the Mexicans would agree to allow the Alamo's defenders to surrender and leave, just as the Texans had allowed Cos to do just two months earlier. The rider, Green Jameson, soon returned with Santa Anna's answer: He would accept nothing less than the unconditional surrender of the Texas stronghold. Bowie's decision to send out Jameson would be his final important command. Travis would make all the decisions from the very first day of the siege.

After the fall of the Alamo, the siege and the brave Texas defenders became part of western legend. Countless works of art, such as this lithograph, have tried to capture the drama and desperation of the fight for the old mission.

Victory or Death

Through the night of February 24, Santa Anna ordered the Mexican artillery into position. That morning, from a distance of 400 yards (366 meters), cannonballs from a pair of nine-pounders (four kilograms) and a five-inch (13-centimeter) howitzer struck the outer walls of the Alamo. That day—the second of the siege—Travis wrote another urgent message to Gonzales, appealing for help. These historical words written by Travis have come to represent the valiant days of the siege as the Texans tried to keep the Mexicans outside the defensive walls of the Alamo:

To the People of Texas & all Americans in the world
Fellow Citizens & Compatriots—I am besieged by a
thousand or more of the Mexicans under Santa Anna—
I have sustained a continual Bombardment & cannonade
for 24 hours & have not lost a man—The Enemy
has demanded a surrender at discretion, otherwise, the
garrison are to be put to the sword, if the fort is taken—
I have answered the demand with a cannon shot, & our
flag still waves proudly from the walls—*I shall never
surrender or retreat. Then, I call on you in the name of
Liberty, of patriotism & everything dear to the American
character, to come to our aid, with all dispatch*—The
enemy is receiving reinforcements daily & will no doubt
increase to three or four thousand in four or five days. If
this call is neglected, I am determined to sustain myself as
long as possible & die like a soldier who never forgets
what is due to his own honor & that of his country—
Victory or Death

Travis underlined the last three words of his stirring
message to the outside world three times. In all, 16 riders
would be sent outside the Alamo fortress during the 13-day
siege with various messages. Yet none of the other messages
portrayed the powerful sentiments this one contained.

During the days that followed, Santa Anna attempted
to put his strategy for bringing about the fall of the Alamo
into effect. He intended to have his men build a series of
entrenchments, or fortified ditches, which would allow the
Mexican forces to move ever closer to the Alamo walls until
a final assault would be launched to breach those walls and
attack the mission's defenders. Even within his own ranks,
Santa Anna's plan had critics. Some Mexican officers
believed it was a mistake to move on the Alamo and lose
time in advancing on the primary target in Texas—the
revolutionary-held garrison in Goliad, 95 miles southeast.

No critics were willing to raise their voices in the face of the driven Mexican general, however.

On February 25, the siege's third day, at 10:00 A.M., the Mexicans launched a limited frontal assault in which 200 to 300 troops moved toward the Alamo. The Texas riflemen beat back the attack with relative ease. The men inside the compound were armed with rifles, including the famous deadly accurate Kentucky rifle. Just about any enemy who came as close as 200 yards (183 meters) away from the Alamo compound was an easy target. The sentries along the perimeter walls often kept four or five rifles loaded at all times. The Mexicans, on the other hand, were firing the smooth-bore "Brown Bess" muskets, which were known for their inaccuracy. (These were the same muskets the British had used against the American patriots during the Revolutionary War.) The fighting resulted in many casualties for the Mexicans, but no loss of life among the Texas defenders.

Santa Anna also attempted to move his men across the San Antonio River and take up positions in a *barrio*, a collection of adobe huts located south and west of the Alamo's walls. This scattering of crude huts, called La Villita, was situated on the Alamo side of the river. It could provide cover for an approach by the Mexican forces. Throughout the day, as they kept up heavy cannon fire aimed at the mission compound, Santa Anna began to move troops into La Villita. From there, he intended to launch an eventual assault. That evening, however, men from inside the Alamo emerged with torches to foil the plan. They set many of the buildings on fire, which took away the cover for the Mexicans. That same night, despite the success of the Texans' strategic move, Travis sent yet another messenger out of the fortress, bound for Gonzales. He pleaded: "It will be impossible for us to keep them [the Mexicans] out much longer. If they overpower us, we fall a sacrifice at the shrine of our country, and we hope posterity and our country will do our memory justice. Give me help, oh my Country!"

The message was carried out of the fortress not by an American defender, but by a Mexican, a *Tejano*, a prominent citizen of San Antonio, Captain Juan Seguín. Since he spoke Spanish, Seguín was able to fool the Mexican picket guards and disappear into the night, riding toward Gonzales on Jim Bowie's horse.

The next day, February 26, it appeared that the besieged garrison at the Alamo might receive help from the Texans who occupied Goliad to the southeast. The Goliad commander, James Fannin, a 32-year-old Georgian, got word that the Mexican army was at San Antonio from the second rider Travis had sent out. Fannin instantly determined to give assistance to the Alamo defenders. He commanded more than 300 men who, late on February 26, prepared to march against the Mexicans stationed outside the Alamo compound. Soon, Fannin led his ill-fated, halfhearted attempt to help the Alamo. Word was sent ahead to San Antonio, and within two days, the Alamo garrison had learned that Fannin and his men were on their way, and that they were bringing four additional cannons with them.

Fannin's march to Béxar went poorly. Just 200 yards (183 meters) out of Goliad, a wagon lost a wheel. Then, two more wagons went down. To make matters worse, the men did not have enough oxen to pull the cannons. Having made little progress, Fannin ordered the men to camp for the night. Overnight, the oxen wandered off, and the rescuers of the Alamo spent the entire day rounding up the livestock. By February 27, the military column had made almost no progress.

Fannin called a council of war. He and his men discussed the pros and cons of continuing the nearly

The Tragic Story of a Loyal Tejano

*A*lthough the majority of the men inside the Alamo were Anglo-Americans, several Tejanos, Mexicans living in Texas, were also present, ready to defend the old mission in the name of the Texas Revolution. The most famous of them was a Mexican rancher named Juan Nepomucena Seguín. His story is one of honor, loyalty, and rejection.

Seguín came from an old Spanish family that had settled in the San Antonio as early as 1722. Raised as the son of a wealthy landowner (his father was mayor of Béxar when Stephen Austin first visited the Texas town), Seguín became interested in politics. In his late twenties, he became the political chief of the San Antonio district. Already on good terms with the Anglo-Americans who were flooding into Texas, Seguín soon became disenchanted with the government in Mexico City and encouraged moves in support of self-government for Texas as an independent state.

When General Cos marched on his hometown, Seguín rallied local Tejano ranchers and fought the Mexican forces. Seguín distinguished himself in the siege to drive Cos from Béxar and was soon appointed as a cavalry captain in the regular Texas army. When Santa Anna's forces arrived in Béxar, Seguín joined the Texans in the Alamo, along with two dozen other Tejanos.

His life might have ended defending the mission, but on February 25, he was sent out by Travis to deliver a message to the Texans at Gonzales. He was able to slip past Mexican sentries by speaking to them in Spanish. When Seguín finally returned to the Alamo, the siege was over. (Later, after the Texas Revolution was over, Seguín would participate in the burial of the remains of those men killed at the Alamo.) This loyal Tejano continued to take part in the revolution, riding with Samuel Houston's army. He fought at the Battle of San Jacinto.

Seguín continued to serve his fellow Texans after the revolution. He held posts in the Texas Senate and as mayor of San Antonio. Sometimes, he had to provide help to fellow Tejanos whose lands were threatened by new arrivals from the United States. Seguín had always envisioned Texas as independent from Mexico, as well as the United States. When Texas drifted toward U.S. statehood, Seguín became a man on the outside. Stories of his disloyalty to Texas began to circulate. By 1842, Sequín was forced to leave the republic and live in Mexico. Only after the Mexican War was Seguín able to return to Texas and live once again in the land he loved so dearly.

100-mile (161-kilometer) march to Béxar. Fannin pointed out that they had few rations and were short on livestock and ammunition. In addition, there were just 320 of them bound for Béxar, where they would have to face a Mexican army that numbered in the thousands. Also, to continue the march would leave Goliad defenseless.

Before the end of February 28, Fannin had ordered his men back to Goliad. The march was abandoned. That same day, both Santa Anna and the Texans inside the Alamo received word of Fannin's planned march. Neither the Mexicans nor the Texans could know that Fannin had already given up his rescue mission.

Even as Fannin's men abandoned their efforts, another unit of Texans made its way to help the Alamo defenders. One of Travis's couriers delivered the garrison commander's message to Gonzales on February 24. Twenty-five men responded to the call and left Gonzales to provide support for the Alamo and its besieged defenders. Along the way, they added seven more men to their number. They arrived at the old Béxar mission on the night of February 29, after they slipped past the Mexicans. The Texans fired on them at the gates of the Alamo, until the new arrivals identified themselves. Unfortunately for the defenders, a few dozen or so new arrivals could not turn the tide of events. This was a fact that Travis and the other men in the compound understood well.

The morning after the 32 reinforcements reached the Alamo, Travis decided to celebrate their arrival by firing two shots from the big 18-pounder. One of the cannon rounds hit Santa Anna's headquarters building in Béxar. The Mexican general was not present.

Seven days had passed since the gates of the mission grounds had been closed in the face of the arriving Mexican army at Béxar. No one inside the mission had been killed, although several Mexicans had fallen, most of them at the hands of the expert riflemen who lined the walls of the Alamo. Still, Santa Anna's forces were not dwindling; in fact, they were increasing. Historian Walter Lord described the mood inside the Texas fortress:

> Monday, February 29, was another gray day, but the norther had given way to a mild, westerly breeze. The men in the Alamo needed it. Worn down by six nights of siege — jittery from the endless shouts and wild bugle calls in the dark — they were bitter and discouraged. Yet they hung on. Partly because, bound together by common peril, none dared to be the first to give in. But another reason lay even deeper. They simply could not shake the conviction that here, above all, was the place to stand. Sooner or later everyone would see it. Meanwhile they must hold out till the rest of Texas woke up.

Day by day, Santa Anna's forces moved closer and closer to the Alamo. Reinforced constantly by additional Mexican arrivals, the front units dug trenches that allowed the Mexican army to inch its way to points within shooting range of the mission grounds. Cannon batteries were established. Mexican artillerymen moved their field pieces behind the new earthworks. Horse patrols explored the perimeter walls, usually at a safe distance from the compound. They had come to know during the first week of siege what happened when one of their number wandered within 200 yards (183 meters) of those Texans armed with their Kentucky long rifles.

Even from their stations outside the walls, the Mexicans became familiar with the rifle work of one of the Alamo's defenders — Davy Crockett. The lanky Tennesseean had brought with him one of his favorite rifles, which he called "Old Betsey," and with it, he made it very difficult for the Mexicans to move south of the mission without drawing his fire. One Mexican captain later described Crockett's deadly work from the palisade wall:

> This man would rest his long gun and fire, and we all learned to keep at a good distance when he was seen to make ready to shoot. He rarely missed his mark, and when he fired he always rose to his feet and calmly reloaded his gun, seemingly indifferent to the shots fired at him by our men. He had a strong, resonant voice and often railed at us. This man I later learned was known as "Kwockey."

Although Davy Crockett was one of the more famous individuals inside the Alamo, modern historians do not have a clear picture of his daily conduct in defending the mission grounds. Stories contradict one another. Travis did mention the frontier congressman in a letter dated February 25, just two days into the siege. As he described the events of a two-hour battle in which Mexican troops attacked the Alamo then retreated under heavy Texan rifle fire, the Alamo's commander wrote: "The Hon. David Crockett was seen at all points, animating the men to do their duty."

Two days after Travis's mention of the famed frontiersman and how he rallied his fellow defenders, Crockett may have fired his Kentucky rifle at Santa Anna himself. The Mexicans had moved a forward cannon battery within rifle range, where the "people in town became convinced that [Crockett] killed the very first soldado to fall, with a two-hundred-yard shot from his long rifle." Late in the day, as Santa Anna rode toward one of the cannon batteries, Alamo riflemen fired at the Mexican general. Here again, "the tejanos in Béxar swore that one of the bullets that sent him scurrying back to safety came from Crockett's rifle." Despite the efforts of such deadly marksmen as Crockett,

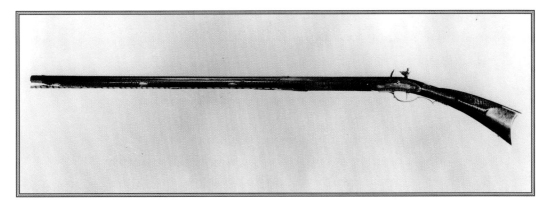

Even though the Texans were hugely outnumbered by the Mexican forces, for 13 days of siege, the Alamo defenders were able to hold off the enemy with the use of long rifles like this one.

the Mexicans were still drawing their artillery positions closer as each day of the siege passed. Repeatedly, Mexican cannon battered the walls of the mission compound.

In time, the men inside the Alamo fell into a regular routine of action, seeing to their daily needs, and refortifying their garrison walls. With each deadly cannon blast, the Texans shored up their defenses, repairing and patching each wall breach as soon as they could find materials. Each man took his turn standing watch on the walls. The various units cooked their meals near their assigned positions, always remaining within sight of the enemy. When the Mexican cannoneers took a rest, so did the men inside the mission. They remained upbeat with one another, and worked hard to keep up the spirits of their comrades. Crockett in particular was remembered for encouraging the men. He even took occasion to play his fiddle while another defender, a Scotsman from Nacogdoches named John McGregor, played the bagpipes. The two men made a point of playing their instruments as loudly as possible. Thanks to the positive mood, many defenders still held out hope that help, rescue, and reinforcements were on their way.

As to reinforcements, the 59 delegates attending the council at Washington-on-the-Brazos did decide on March 2, at the same time they voted for independence, to dispatch Sam Houston with volunteers to aid the men inside the Alamo. Houston decided to make his way to the Alamo on March 6, four days later.

Travis saw this continuing optimism among his men. He mentioned it on March 3, when he sent out another courier to deliver a message to the council at Washington-on-the-Brazos. Travis did not know that the council had already voted for Texas independence the previous day, or that the politics of the revolution had changed the future. Inside the Alamo, the Texans continued to fly the orange-white-and-green-striped flag in support of the Mexican Constitution of 1824. The March 3 dispatch was to be Travis's last message to the outside world. His assessment of his men and their circumstances was a combination of military reporting, the honorable expressions of a proud commander, a promise to extract a high cost at the enemy's expense, and a prophecy of victory for a newly independent Texas:

> At least two hundred shells have fallen inside of our works without having injured a single man; indeed, we have been so fortunate as not to lose a man from any cause, and we have killed many of the enemy. The spirits of my men are still high. . . . I look to the colonies alone for aid; unless it arrives soon, I shall have to fight the enemy on his own terms. I will, however, do the best I can and I feel confident that the determined valor and desperate courage heretofore exhibited by my men will not fail them . . . the victory will cost the enemy so dear, that it will be worse for him than defeat. I hope your honorable body will hasten reinforcements. . . . Our supply of ammunition is limited. . . . God and Texas. Victory or Death.

Ten days of siege had passed by March 3, and the Mexican commander, Santa Anna, was ready to bring the siege to a swift and deadly end for the Texan defenders inside the Alamo. San Antonio and its mission fortress had not figured highly in Santa Anna's original plans for the invasion of Texas. He had recognized the strategic position of Béxar and had intended to take it over with little time and trouble. He had not reckoned on the stubborn strength of the mission's defenders. Santa Anna had rushed to Béxar only on his way to somewhere else, to the eastern portion of Texas, where he would get rid of opposition and rebellion all the way to Nacogdoches. He was wasting time in Béxar. Every day his troops spent hammering down the defensive walls of the mission was another day that delayed the ultimate victory of his campaign to crush the Texas Revolution.

Although the situation looked bleak for the Alamo defenders by early March, many corners of Texas were actually stirring on their behalf. Travis's letter of February 24 had not only reached Fannin and his 300 men at Goliad, but also others who were made aware of Travis's desperate need for help. At Victoria, a group of Texans crossed the Guadalupe River, bound for the Alamo. In San Felipe, south of Washington-on-the-Brazos, a local militia unit, under the command of Captain Moseley Baker marched toward Béxar on February 29. There was general excitement across the Texas colonies when the word came that the 32 men from Gonzales had already made it inside the walls of the mission. Others talked of Fannin's mission of more than 300 rescuers, not knowing that Fannin had given up on the venture and returned to Goliad. Other rescuers were recruited in smaller bands. They set out, bound for Béxar, intent on helping their besieged brethren at the Alamo. Juan Seguín, the Mexican rancher Travis had sent out as a courier, was also on his way back, with 25 pro-revolutionary Mexicans at his side. By March 1, even

Juan Seguín, a Mexican aristocrat, joined the Texas revolutionaries in the fight for independence. He survived the battle for the Alamo, because Travis sent him out as a messenger before the Mexican army made its attack.

Fannin was again planning to march to the Alamo. The next day, he and 200 of his men prepared to leave for Béxar, intending to "march tomorrow or next day, if we can procure fresh oxen enough to transport our baggage and two 6-pounders." Yet even as Fannin and his men got ready to march once again, for the men inside the Alamo, the needed reinforcements were already long overdue.

Late in the evening of March 3, a rider emerged in the safety of the Alamo's walls. It was one of Travis's couriers, James Butler Bonham, a dark-haired 28-year-old whom Travis had sent out on two message deliveries, one on February 16 and one on February 27. Bonham did not bring good news. Fannin, it seemed, was not coming. (Bonham was not aware of Fannin's revived plans for a second march.) Other reinforcements might be on their way, but not Fannin and his several hundred loyal Texans, on whom the defenders had been relying.

Travis prepared to send out another courier. That night, several of the men inside the Alamo, feeling uncertain about their fate, wrote personal notes of their own to be delivered to friends and loved ones. Travis sent one such message to a woman in San Felipe. To a friend who was taking care of Travis's young son, he wrote: "Take care of my little boy. If the country should be saved, I may make him a splendid fortune; but if the country should be lost and I should perish, he will have nothing but the proud recollection that he is the son of a man who died for his country." To another acquaintance, Travis penned: "Let the convention go on and make a declaration of independence . . . and the world will understand what we are fighting for."

As the morning of Friday, March 4, dawned, the men inside the Alamo did not feel that the end was at hand. In fact, however, the noose was closing in on them. Mexican gun emplacements had been moved to within 250 yards (229 meters) of the Alamo's walls, and the cannonballs were able to strike the fortress's north wall with unrelenting accuracy. The defenders worked feverishly to repair or refill these new breaches.

The situation was beginning to look grim. Davy Crockett, usually an optimistic, even cheerful voice among the defenders, was starting to feel the strain of being unable to get away from the threat of Mexican guns. He spoke to some of his colleagues: "I think we had better march out and die in the open air. I don't like to be hemmed up."

Jim Bowie was still alive, despite his desperate illness. He was of little help, though. Occasionally during the siege, he was brought out of his sick room in the Low Barracks, near the palisade defended by Davy Crockett and his fellow Tennesseeans. Exactly what illness Bowie was suffering from remains unclear. Some historians believe it was pneumonia, while others say it might have been typhoid fever or tuberculosis. Whatever it was, Bowie appeared to be dying from it. At times, he was carried about the garrison compound on a litter, to help encourage the men. Other than that, Bowie played no military role during the siege. On the morning of March 4, Bowie was again carried out of his sick room to bolster the lagging spirits of the men.

Throughout the day on March 4, an ominous cloud hung over the besieged. Some of the Mexican guns were now just 200 yards (183 meters) from the exterior compound walls. New Mexican troops were being deployed in Béxar, seemingly preparing for action. Three new battalions had arrived since the siege began, which brought Santa Anna's number of troops to more than 3,000. Despite the fact that the 12-pounders (5 kilograms) had not yet arrived, Santa Anna was ready for an attack on the Alamo. Soon the signs could be seen by the men inside the fortress: The Mexican troops were building scaling ladders.

The events of the day may have been extremely discouraging to the Anglo–American defenders, but the Mexicans who had sided with the Texans were beginning to rethink their loyalties. They had, after all, joined with the Texans to fight for Mexican statehood and on behalf of the Mexican Constitution of 1824. Those issues were now moot. Texas had declared its independence. Some of the Mexicans wondered what future they could possibly expect in a Texas that was dominated by Anglo–Americans. Some of those who had joined the revolutionaries had friends in Béxar; some even had friends and relatives in Santa Anna's army. Thus, throughout the day, some of the Mexicans inside the Alamo quietly slipped out of the compound and made their way to Béxar.

At least one of these people, a Mexican woman, went to Santa Anna himself and told him about the conditions inside the compound. She reported that there was low ammunition and crumbling walls. It was an opportunity for success if the Mexican army would storm the Alamo. Santa Anna knew he had the Alamo defenders with their backs to the wall. His cannons were already in position in the field, already destroying the walls of the Alamo fortress. Larger cannons, 12-pounders, were on the way, just two or three days from Béxar. For the proud Mexican general, the end of the siege was near.

Inside the Alamo, Travis was tempted to consider either surrender or, possibly, escape into the night, out of harm's way, for him and his men. Escape would not be a dishonorable alternative. Even West Point manuals of the day offered advice on when to consider escape for militia officers in field fortifications, such as Travis at the Alamo. The guidelines said: "in an isolated post, if the enemy, after having been repulsed, makes a show of blockading it, or of renewing his attack, and there is no prospect of succor arriving, the garrison should attempt an escape by night."

On the evening of March 5, Travis spoke to his men, making the situation as clear as he could. After the siege was over, only one man who had been present at Travis's presentation was alive to tell the story, a Frenchman named Louis Moses Rose. Perhaps a veteran of the Napoleonic wars, Rose—who was later identified by others by the name "Ross"—chose to escape from the Alamo that night, leaving his comrades inside the fortress. For his own personal reasons, he did not choose, when presented with an option by Travis, to remain inside the garrison and be killed. By his account, Travis approached the men and spoke to them plainly about their options. (Unfortunately, Rose's version was later retold through another party, whose son finally wrote down Travis's speech. No one can be certain of the accuracy of the words ascribed to Travis.) The record of Travis's speech includes the following:

> My brave companions, I must come to the point. Our fate is sealed. Within a very few days—perhaps a very few hours—we must all be in eternity. This is our destiny, and we cannot avoid it. This is our certain doom. I have deceived you long by the promise of help. But I crave your pardon . . . in deceiving you, I also deceived myself, having been first deceived by others.

Travis continued, explaining that help was not going to arrive. He noted the size of the Mexican army that stood outside the gates of the Alamo. He spoke of the possibilities of escape and surrender, but made it clear that he hoped they would all stay and fight. Travis informed them that every man was free to make his own decision about whether to remain or leave. As for him, Travis assured them, regardless of everyone else's decisions, he would defend the Alamo even if it meant fighting alone. Then, Travis took out his sword and walked across the garrison grounds, dragging his weapon in the dirt to draw a line. Such a gesture would be familiar to men like those who occupied the Alamo. Some of them had already crossed such a line in the past. It was a common practice among militia officers to draw lines or do something similar to give their troops an opportunity to "vote with their feet."

The first to cross the line, according to the story told later by Rose, was a 26-year-old named Tapley Holland, whose father had fought in the War of 1812. Shortly, every man standing, except one, crossed the line. Those who were sick or wounded struggled from their cots and stepped across. Jim Bowie, lying on his bed, called out to those around him: "Boys, I am not able to come to you, but I wish some of you would be so kind as to remove my cot over there." Four men sprang forward and helped Bowie across Travis's line. Only one, 50-year-old Louis Rose, elected to follow a different path. As he made his choice clear, Crockett is alleged to have said to him, "You may as well conclude to die with us, old man, for escape is impossible." With this symbolic gesture of intent, the men inside the Alamo sealed their own fates. Now, regardless of how the siege might end, the die was cast. They would remain inside the mission compound and face the inevitable.

The Mexicans
Are Coming

This 1905 painting by Henry Arthur McArdle shows the brave spirit of the Alamo's defenders. In his attempt to capture the full drama of the battle, the artist has depicted a ghostly figure intended to be the spirit of Jim Bowie, who was sick in bed during the siege and could not take part in the fighting.

By the evening of March 5, the twelfth day of the siege, the end was near. At 10:00 P.M., the day-long Mexican bombardment came to a sudden halt. Men who had remained at their posts along the Alamo's perimeter walls almost immediately began to fall asleep. Even Travis took a short rest on his cot, his sword and a double-barreled shotgun at his side. After a week and a half of nearly endless strain and assault, the men inside the Alamo were tired beyond comparison.

Outside, across the treeless plains of San Antonio de Béxar, opposite the San Antonio River, General Santa Anna was drinking a cup of coffee and preparing his men for their great assault on the Alamo compound. Four columns of infantrymen, with 800 men in

101

each column, would lead the attack. Two columns would attack the northeast and northwest perimeter corners. A third would make an assault on the east wall, at the rear of the mission church, while the fourth would strike at the Alamo's most vulnerable spot: the wooden palisade wall that had been constructed in front of the mission church, where Davy Crockett had stood his ground throughout the siege. Hundreds of Mexican cavalrymen would hold back and wait for any Alamo defenders who might try to escape the grounds. Approximately 4,000 Mexican troops were ready for the assault on the Alamo, which was defended by fewer than 200 men.

All had been carefully prepared for the attack. Near midnight, the Mexican officers began to wake their men and ready them for the last thrust of the siege. An hour later, the various military units were advancing. It was now the early morning of Sunday, March 6. Each of the attackers was armed with a musket and 10 shots. Some of the soldiers carried tools, including picks, axes, crowbars, and spikes. Others carried scaling ladders. Over the next three hours, thousands of Mexican soldiers moved into position as quietly as they could. It was a dark night, with heavy clouds blocking the light of the moon. By 4:00 A.M., most of the troops were in place, crouching in the damp, dewy grass, and waiting for their opportunity to bring down the men inside the Alamo.

Near 5:00 A.M., just as the dim light of the dawn scattered its feeble rays across the open ground surrounding the Alamo, the voice of a Mexican soldier broke the stillness: *Viva [long live] Santa Anna!*" The shrill yet stirring notes of a bugle signaled the attack. Through the shadows came the charge of thousands of Mexican soldiers, all with the same objective: the fall of the Alamo. Then came the sound of a different bugle call, the Deguello, an old Spanish song from medieval times.

The siege of the Alamo went on for 13 days before the Mexican army finally began its attack on the compound, early on the morning of March 6.

Deguello meant "cut throat," and the bugle call had come to signify death in the bullring. The Deguello was ordered by Santa Anna, even though nearly all the Mexican troops would have been unfamiliar with the tune. Whether they knew the song or not, it indicated the intent of the Mexican general: to take no prisoners and give no quarter.

A Texan captain on the Alamo walls shouted out the cry that woke many of his colleagues in arms: "Colonel Travis! The Mexicans are coming!" Quickly, Travis was on his feet, grabbing his weapons as he ran to take his position along the north wall. Travis shouted to his men: "Come on boys, the Mexicans are upon us and we'll give them Hell!"

Inside the Alamo, the men scrambled anxiously to their posts. Infantrymen streamed out of their barracks and manned the parapets. The gunners emerged from the Long Barracks and took to their guns. Soon the 12-pounders were blasting away into the night, illuminating the corners of the compound grounds that the early morning sun could not reach. The cannons, however, could not hit the Mexicans who had already reached the ground below the walls. There, Santa Anna's men began to make their first efforts at erecting scaling ladders against the outer wall of the Alamo.

From his position at the emplacement of a pair of 8-pounders, along the north wall, William Travis fired his shotgun down toward the approaching Mexican soldiers. Then, suddenly, with the battle barely under way, an unknown enemy soldier fired his weapon, hitting the Alamo's commander in the head. Travis dropped his gun outside the wall as he toppled down the cannon emplacement. He was not killed instantly. He rolled into an upright position on the ground of the Alamo compound. It was there that he would bleed to death. Travis, in fact, may have been the first Anglo-American killed in the entire course of the 13-day siege.

With Mexican forces pressing the fight from every direction, the Alamo's defenders fought valiantly. Despite Santa Anna's plan, the men inside the mission compound were not about to hand the Mexican general an easy victory. Historian David Nevin described the hard-fighting tenacity of the Texans:

> The attack did not go well. The column striking from the east was pinned by the murderous shot from the cannon on the church, and Crockett's men and the small guns on the palisade blew back the column assigned to take the south wall. On the north side, a few Mexicans reached the walls, safe from the Texas cannon which could not depress to reach them. But the bulk of both northern columns stopped and milled . . . The Mexican officers whipped their men forward with the flats of their sabers. They came on again and for the second time, the withering sheets of grape [shot] and rifle fire turned them. On the third thrust the column coming to

the northwest corner drifted to the east. The eastern column, held down by fire, drifted to the north, and both merged with the northeast column. Now all three columns—a single mass of men, the front rows falling like grass before the scythe—came surging to the walls of the Alamo.

By now, the battle just fifteen minutes into the assault, with Mexican troops massed at the foot of the Alamo's walls, the two dozen or so scaling ladders were nowhere in sight. They had been trampled in the confusion, and were already lying in pieces on the cold morning ground.

On the opposite side of the walls, the Texans struggled to hold back the ever-increasing numbers of Mexican troops. Santa Anna had already sent in his reserve forces, including his grenadiers and his unit of engineers, known as the *Zapadores*. The Mexicans were jammed so tightly together that some of them, as they shot the heavy Brown Bess muskets that fired a .75-caliber lead ball, accidentally shot at the heads of the other Mexican soldiers in front of them. In fact, before the battle was over, more Mexicans would be killed by "friendly fire"—bullets fired by their own men, than by the Texan defenders.

A Mexican officer, José Enrique de la Pena, observed the confusion of the massed Mexican troops along the north wall and wrote a description in his diary: "A quarter of an hour had elapsed, during which our soldiers remained in a terrible situation, wearing themselves out as they climbed in quest of a less obscure death than that visited on them, crowded in a single mass." Perhaps as many as 1,500 troops pressed along the wall. Hundreds lay dead.

Meanwhile, at the southern perimeter of the Alamo grounds, Colonel Juan Morales's fourth column was making a broad attack toward the south wall and the wooden palisade where Davy Crockett and his fellow Tennesseeans were positioned. The initial Mexican attack was pushed back by Crockett and his men. As the Mexicans thrust forward for a second advance, they concentrated their efforts away from the deadly accuracy of the Tennessee riflemen, and moved toward the south-west corner of the wall. Here, the 18-pounder, at least for a while, did its deadly work. Then, just as had happened on the north wall, the Mexican troops were able to come in close enough to the wall itself that they were no longer in range of the cannon. As Morales's men hit this portion of the wall, they met little rifle fire. Several of the defenders had already rushed to the north wall to help

The Mystery of Crockett's Death

Even though Davy Crockett was one of the most famous Americans inside the Alamo, a mystery surrounds his death even today: How did it happen? The answer to this question is shrouded in speculation, misinformation, storytelling, and legend-making.

The many versions of his death may be categorized into the following possibilities: 1) He was killed during the chaotic fighting that took place within the mission grounds after the Mexicans gained entry into the Alamo; 2) He was killed while trying to escape from the Alamo compound, as did many of his comrades, once the Mexicans began to go systematically door-to-door to rout the Texans who had taken refuge in the barracks; or 3) He was taken prisoner with a handful of other Texans and executed by the direct order of Santa Anna. Each of these stories has been presented as truth by various "eyewitnesses" of the events that took place on that fateful day inside the Alamo. Obviously, however, not all of the stories can be true, and unfortunately, none of them can be believed without doubts.

One of the more recent revelations to describe the death of Davy Crockett came down in the form of Mexican Lieutenant José Enrique de la Pena's diary. In 1975, the diary was published in the United States. According to de la Pena, Crockett and a few other men were taken prisoner following the early morning battle. When they were presented to Santa Anna, he instantly their comrades. This left the southwest wall under-protected. As the Mexicans stormed forward, the unthinkable occurred. The 18-pounder fell into their hands. After the annihilation of the cannon crew, Mexican soldiers poured down the cannon embankment, finding themselves in the southern yard of the mission compound. They swept toward the north wall from inside the Alamo grounds, while other units from each of the four original Mexican columns were also making their way over the walls.

As the Mexicans began to fill the compound, great confusion and a frenzy of action and death reigned. Mexican soldiers met Texans in hand-to-hand combat.

became angry that any prisoners had been spared and ordered them killed. According to the diary, Crockett and the others were bayoneted and shot. Despite the possible truth of the account, these particular pages of de la Pena's diary have been called into question by modern historians, most notably Alamo writer, Bill Groneman, who believes the de la Pena journal is a forgery.

Perhaps historian William C. Davis has stated the mystery of Crockett's death in its simplest form, leaving the curious with no definite answers, simply because irrefutable explanations are difficult to come by:

He may have died fighting at the palisade, or in the redoubt on the west wall, or out in the chaparral, or being brutally executed after he was disarmed. We simply do not know, and—unsatisfactory as it is for those impelled to have a definite answer—we probably never will. The irony should not go without note: That the most famous man inside the Alamo, a man who embodied many of the ideals for which the Texans fought, died alongside them, without notice.

One thing can be said with certainty. If Crockett was executed following his capture, then the record of what happened to his body is clear. Santa Anna ordered the Alamo corpses to be placed on three pyres, along with dry firewood. Flammable camphene was poured over the dead and ignited.

The Mexican officer, de la Pena, wrote of the action in his diary:

> But disorder had already begun; officers of all ranks shouted but were hardly heard. The most daring of our veterans tried to be the first to climb . . . yelling wildly so that room could be made for them, at times climbing over their own comrades . . . A lively rifle fire coming from the roof of the barracks and other points caused painful havoc, increasing the confusion of our disorderly mass. The first to climb were thrown down by bayonets already waiting for them behind the parapet, or by pistol fire, but the courage of our soldiers was not diminished as they saw their comrades falling dead or wounded, and they hurried to occupy their places and to avenge them, climbing over their bleeding bodies. The sharp retorts of the rifles, the whistling of bullets, the groans of the wounded, the cursing of the men, the sighs and anguished cries of the dying. . . . the noise of the instruments of war, and the inordinate shouts of the attackers, who climbed vigorously, bewildered all and made of this moment a tremendous and critical one. The shouting of those being attacked was no less loud and from the beginning had pierced our ears with desperate, terrible cries of alarm in a language we did not understand.

With so many Mexicans on Alamo grounds, there were additional casualties among them caused by "friendly fire." As a swirl of Mexican combatants filled the Alamo mission grounds, the Texans retreated to the various rooms of the barracks, taking up defensive positions. Before the battle, they had cut loopholes in the walls through which they could fire their rifles. Still, they knew they were firing despite the fates that awaited them. Victory for the Mexicans was sealed. The battle was nearly over.

Although most of the Mexicans had been armed well enough before the battle to fire their muskets as many as eight to ten times during the assault on the Alamo, once inside, many of them began to use their weapon of advantage: the bayonet. The Texans' rifles were not designed to hold bayonets, but the models carried by the Mexicans were. Santa Anna expected his men to use them, giving instructions that "the arms, principally the bayonets, should be in perfect order." The Texans, with low ammunition or no time to reload their rifles, were forced to use various knives, including Bowie and butcher knives. Otherwise, they used their rifles as clubs. Mexican soldiers moved from room to room, killing Texans and sometimes being killed themselves. Morales and his men then turned the 18-pounder toward the barracks and began to blast the hiding places of the last of the Texas combatants to pieces.

As the number of Texans was slowly reduced, one defender, the artillery commander named Almaron Dickinson, rushed into the roofless church where his wife, Susannah, and their young child were hiding. In a rush, he spoke his last words to her: "Great God, Sue, the Mexicans are inside our walls! All is lost! If they spare you, save my child." Then he kissed her one last time, as he drew his sword from its sheath, and exited into the Alamo courtyard. There, he was killed. Most of the Texans killed in the Alamo died in the Long Barracks. Some of the cannon blasts actually killed Mexicans as well as Texans.

A few of the Texans tried to surrender. They waved white flags on the ends of their rifles or even used their own socks. However, if one man in a room might have wanted to surrender, others might not. As a result, some Mexicans entered rooms expecting to find a vanquished enemy, only to be shot and killed. As de la Pena described it: "Some with an accent hardly intelligible, desperately cried Mercy, valiant Mexicans; others poked the points of their bayonets

Susannah Dickinson was the wife of Texan defender Almaron Dickinson. She and her child survived the battle for the old mission and were able to tell the tale of the annihilation of the Alamo.

through a hole or a door with a white cloth, the symbol of cease-fire." When the Mexicans were fired upon, de la Pena continued: "Thus betrayed, our men rekindled their anger and at every moment fresh skirmishes broke out with renewed fury. The order had been given to spare no one but the women and this was carried out, but such carnage was useless and had we prevented it, we would have saved much blood on our part."

In the midst of the massacre described by de la Pena, the Mexican troops seemed to move about the Alamo grounds in a bloody overkill. Texans were shot repeatedly and received multiple bayonet stabs. According to one Mexican record, one Alamo defender "was pierced by not less than twenty bayonets." Even the dead were stuck repeatedly with Mexican bayonets, perhaps to make certain they were dead, but seemingly because no live victims could be found. Corpses were shot; bodies of Texans were mutilated by Mexican troops, followed by a general search of their clothing for valuables. At one point, a stray cat was shot. A Mexican soldier explained, "it is not a cat, but an American."

With orders to kill all combatants, the Mexicans even annihilated the sick and wounded. Among these victims was the incapacitated Jim Bowie. Exactly how Bowie died during the attack on the Alamo remains a mystery. Various versions of his death were given after the fact, some by Anglo witnesses, others by Mexican soldiers. Several versions described Bowie as firing shots to kill Mexicans before he was killed. Others claim that he died "like a woman, hidden almost under a mattress." Susannah Dickinson recounted his death in two different stories. In one, she said Bowie was shot in the head, his brains splattering on the adobe walls of his sick room. Bowie's sister-in-law, who was also present during the siege, later described how Mexican soldiers "tossed Bowie's body on their bayonets until his blood covered their clothes and dyed them red." One story even stated that he was dead before the attack began. All the stories tend to agree on only one point: Bowie was not able to leave his sickbed before he died.

Once the Mexicans had cleared the barracks of the last defender, they attacked the final stronghold inside the Alamo grounds: the mission church. There, the women and children had hidden during the battle. Infantrymen broke down the main church door and soon filled the ruined building, searching for any remaining Texans. The few who had taken refuge there were soon found and killed on the spot, sometimes in front of the cowering women. As for the women, they were not harmed and were allowed to go free. Children were also spared, as well as a Mexican male who told the victorious troops he had been held in the Alamo against his will. Only one other man inside the Alamo survived: Travis's slave, Joe.

By this point, above the roofless sanctuary, the morning sun had dawned. The time was 6:30 A.M. The battle had taken only 90 minutes. The Mexicans had been able to breach the walls of the Alamo within the first 20 minutes of the attack.

All the defenders of the Alamo were either killed or soon would be. According to one Mexican officer: "The enemy loss was [complete], that is to say 183." Among the last to face death were five men, who, according to Mexican sources, were brought before Santa Anna as prisoners. The general made it clear to his men there were to be no prisoners, thus, the last of the Alamo's defenders were immediately executed.

Later that same day, Sunday, March 6, the Mexicans gathered wood from the nearby trees. About mid-afternoon, they began to place the dead bodies of Texans on the wood. The bodies of the men who had defended the Alamo did not receive honorable burials; instead, they were burned.

In the end, General Santa Anna did not even consider his victory over the Texans at the Alamo a major military action. He referred to it as "a small affair." Yet his losses included approximately 1,500 dead, a figure equal to about one out of every three soldiers who took part in the attack. More than 400 Mexican soldiers had been

Even though the bodies of the Texan defenders were burned without receiving an honorable burial, they were later honored with a marble monument that included statues of some of the leaders of the fight.

wounded during the attack. Santa Anna had many of his men buried in and around Béxar, but when the cemetery was filled to capacity, he had dozens of his own dead tossed into the San Antonio River.

Will You Come
to the Bower?

The Mexicans destroyed the Texan defenders at the Alamo, but when Sam Houston and his Texas army set out to fight back, the tide was turned. At the Battle of San Jacinto, the Texans routed the Mexican army, and Santa Anna was forced to surrender.

Though the Alamo victory seemed to be of little consequence to Santa Anna, the loss of the old Béxar mission would hit the Texans hard. The Texas military leader, Sam Houston, received word of the Alamo's fall less than a week later, on March 11. He was in Gonzales when two Mexicans arrived with news that the defenders at the Alamo had failed. Two days later, Susannah Dickinson, who had been released by Santa Anna so she could tell the story of the Alamo's defeat, arrived in Gonzales. There, she met with Houston and gave him her version of the siege. Despite the disappointment, anguish, and anger the Texans felt as they heard the news of the annihilation of the Alamo's forces, Houston was in no immediate position to avenge the loss of the mission that he had ordered Travis and Bowie to abandon weeks earlier. Prepared or not, Houston now knew that he would soon face the threat of Santa Anna's advancing army.

The siege had been a costly one for the Mexican leader, however. The combination of the marksmanship of the Texas riflemen, the friendly fire suffered by Mexicans during the attack, and the large number of desertions within the Mexican army, left Santa Anna in the field with approximately 2,000 men. Still, despite his reduced numbers, Santa Anna was certain of himself and his ultimate victory over the ragtag Texas forces. He divided his army into two forces, intending to speed up the destruction of all Texas resistance.

While a third army of 1,400 men, under the command of General José Francisco Urrea, drove up from the south toward Goliad, Santa Anna sent General Antonio Gaona northeast with 700 men toward the community of Bastrop, then southeast toward San Felipe. Meanwhile, Santa Anna and General Joaquín Ramírez y Sesma led 1,200 troops through the heart of the Texas colonies.

A repeat of the Alamo defeat took place at Goliad, where General Urrea engaged Colonel Fannin's 400 men after the Mexican general had caught up with Fannin just six miles outside of the town. Outnumbered by more than 1,000 of the enemy, Fannin's men fought well for two days, holed up in a circle of wagons. They killed 250 Mexican troops, with only seven men of their own killed. Fannin was wounded in the leg. On March 20, the remaining Texans surrendered to Urrea, after he promised to allow them to leave Texas for the United States. After being held as prisoners for eight days, receiving humane treatment from General Urrea, however, word arrived from Santa Anna that all the captives from the Goliad engagement were to be executed. On

March 27, the Texans were gathered together. They soon faced a surprise firing squad made up of hundreds of Mexican troops. Most of the captives were killed on the spot. Several dozen did manage to escape, running for their lives into the surrounding marshes. In all, 371 Texans were slaughtered that day. The massacre gave rise to a second battle cry for the surviving Texas loyalists: "Remember the Alamo! Remember Goliad!"

After two devastating defeats within three weeks, many Texas families began to flee their lands. Panic spread across Texas, as Houston seemed unable to meet the enemy successfully in the field. Houston simply lacked enough men to engage Santa Anna's forces directly. Repeatedly, as Mexican forces approached his army, Houston retreated, hoping to face the enemy another day. Gradually, new Texan recruits—some of them recent arrivals from Louisiana, Mississippi, and Kentucky—joined his army. By April, Houston was in command of approximately 1,000 men. An American army did gather along the border of Texas as well, but it remained on U.S. soil and offered no direct support to the beleaguered Texans.

As Houston's forces slowly increased in number, Santa Anna's forces dwindled, largely through desertion. In addition, the Mexican general was now deep in Texas, in hostile enemy territory, and his supply lines were overextended. To make matters worse, he had divided his forces. The Texas situation was not entirely optimistic, despite their reinforcements. As Houston continued to avoid a military confrontation with Santa Anna's larger force, some of the Texas commander's men also deserted, frustrated with Houston's apparent inability to make a stand against the Mexicans. By April 20, Houston's army had only about 800 men left. Santa Anna's army, newly strengthened by the arrival of General Cos's men, numbered near 1,300.

Finding Santa Anna's men along the San Jacinto River, Houston finally decided to attack on April 21, at 4:30 P.M., just after the Mexicans had taken the saddles off their horses and prepared to take their *siesta* (afternoon rest). (Houston had placed men in the trees where they could see the enemy camp and keep the Texas commander informed of the status of the Mexican troops.) With the Mexican muskets stacked and the mass of enemy troops asleep, including Santa Anna, Houston ordered an assault.

As quietly as they could, Houston's men crept forward. Recent rains helped mask the sounds of horse hooves, although the mud slowed the progress of the artillery-men, who heaved under the weight of a pair of cannons they called the Twin Sisters. There was no martial music, no fife or drum to awaken the enemy. As soon as the cannons were in place just 200 yards (183 meters) from the Mexican encampment, Houston commanded his men to open fire. Only then did Texas drums roll and fifes peal out, as the fifers began to play their favorite song, "Will You Come to the Bower?" Cries of "Remember the Alamo!" and "Remember Goliad!" filled the air, resonating off the sharp blasts that belched from the pair of angry cannons.

The battle was chaotic and quick. One of the Texans, a nephew of Stephen Austin's named Moses Austin Bryan, later wrote of what he saw: "The most awful slaughter I ever saw was when the Texans pursued the retreating Mexicans, killing on all sides, even the wounded . . . I had a double-barrel shotgun and had shot only four times when we crossed the breastworks. After that I shot no more at the poor devils who were running." Among those who fled the field was Santa Anna himself. One of his own men described the general's retreat: "I saw his Excellency running about in the utmost excitement, wringing his hands and unable to give an order."

The final fight for Texas independence had been decisive. Houston's men caught the Mexicans completely off-guard. Although the Battle of San Jacinto lasted little more than 18 minutes, the casualty figures were lopsided, indicating a major victory for Houston. Six hundred Mexicans were killed during the battle and another 650 were taken as prisoners. For the Texans, only 23 were wounded and two men were killed. After eluding capture through the night of April 21–22, Santa Anna was caught by a Texas patrol and brought to Houston.

Despite his defeat, the captured Santa Anna remained vain. He met Houston under a tree, where the Texas commander, having suffered a wound to his leg during the engagement, was lying on a blanket. As Santa Anna approached, he took a pinch of opium from his medicine box. Then he said within earshot of Houston: "That man may consider himself born to no common destiny who has conquered the Napoleon of the West . . . And now it remains for him to be generous to the vanquished."

Houston's response was clear and to the point. It literally caused the defeated Mexican general to shake in fear. Houston said: "You should have remembered that at the Alamo."

Santa Anna's life was spared. He was forced to sign a peace agreement called the Treaty of Velasco. In it, he promised to remove his troops and to recognize the independence of Texas. Within weeks, U.S. President Andrew Jackson recognized the newly formed and independent Republic of Texas. Santa Anna returned to Mexico, where he repudiated the agreement, claiming he had only accepted the peace treaty under threat of his life.

Despite Santa Anna's stubbornness, Texas was to be free and independent of any future Mexican threat. Hundreds of loyal Texans had died during the months-long conflict with

Sam Houston, the victorious general in the Battle of San Jacinto, went on to become president of the independent Republic of Texas. He is seen here entering the newly founded city of Houston in 1837.

powerful Mexico. Even to this day, many of those who risked their lives, their families' security, and their future fortunes are still remembered for the role they played in winning independence for Texas. Perhaps best remembered among them are the gallant men who stared death in the face when they crossed a line drawn along the dry earth of the mission compound of the Alamo.

1500s	Following the voyages of Columbus, Spain begins to establish colonies in Central and South America and the Caribbean Islands.
1530s	Shipwrecked Spaniard, Álvar Núñez Cabeza de Vaca, washes up on shores of modern-day Texas; after his return to Mexico City, he inspires others to explore the region.
1540s	Spanish explorers Hernando de Soto and Francisco Vásquez de Coronado separately explore regions of modern-day Texas.
1688–1690	Spanish governor of Coahuila, Don Alonso de León, establishes a mission along the Trinity River of East Texas.
1716	French-Canadian Louis de St. Denis and his followers establish a series of rival missions and forts, including one at Nacogdoches on the Red River.
1718	Spanish governor of Coahuila, Martín de Alarcón, establishes a settlement along the banks of the San Antonio River, erecting a fort called the Presidio of San Antonio de Béxar; near the Spanish fortress, a Catholic friar establishes a church, the Mission of San Antonio de Valero, which would one day be called the Alamo.

1730
Mission-fort community
of San Antonio de Bexar
falls under attack by
band of Lipan Apache

1718
Spanish establish fort
at San Antonio River,
Mission of San Antonio
de Valero built (Alamo)

1763
Spanish gain control of
Louisiana and ultimately
allow non-Spanish
peoples to settle there

1700

1790

1786
Americans are
allowed entrance into
Spanish Louisiana

Timeline

1730   Mission-fort community of San Antonio de Béxar falls under attack by a band of Lipan Apache.

1763   French lose all claims to the western lands of Louisiana under the treaty ending the French and Indian War (Seven Years' War); Louisiana comes under Spanish control.

1780s   Spanish authorities invite non-Spanish residents into Louisiana Territory, including Germans, French, and British.

1786   Americans are allowed entrance into Spanish Louisiana.

1790s   The total Spanish population in Texas amounts to fewer than 3,000 people, including American Indians.

1800   King of Spain abruptly halts the flow of Americans into his northern colonies; that same year, French ruler Napoleon Bonaparte forces the Spanish king to grant him ownership of the vast Louisiana region; before year's end, a plot to seize Texas from Spain is launched by a group of Americans, led by Philip Nolan; the attempt fails and Nolan is killed.

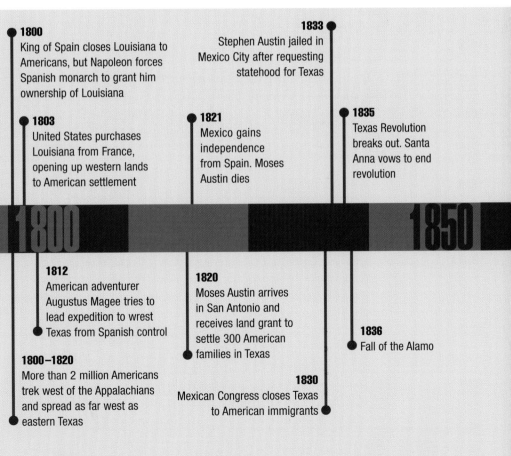

1800
King of Spain closes Louisiana to Americans, but Napoleon forces Spanish monarch to grant him ownership of Louisiana

1833
Stephen Austin jailed in Mexico City after requesting statehood for Texas

1803
United States purchases Louisiana from France, opening up western lands to American settlement

1821
Mexico gains independence from Spain. Moses Austin dies

1835
Texas Revolution breaks out. Santa Anna vows to end revolution

1800

1850

1812
American adventurer Augustus Magee tries to lead expedition to wrest Texas from Spanish control

1820
Moses Austin arrives in San Antonio and receives land grant to settle 300 American families in Texas

1836
Fall of the Alamo

1800–1820
More than 2 million Americans trek west of the Appalachians and spread as far west as eastern Texas

1830
Mexican Congress closes Texas to American immigrants

1803	United States purchases the Louisiana Territory from the French, opening up the lands west of the Mississippi River to American settlement.
1812	Another American adventurer, Augustus Magee, launches a plot to take Texas away from Spanish control; this plot, too, fails; Magee is killed after his capture.
1800–1820	More than 2 million Americans trek west of the Appalachian Mountains and spread out as far west as the northern and eastern borders of Texas.
1819	Spanish surrender control of Florida to the United States under the Adams-Onís Treaty.
1820	Spanish population of Texas stands at fewer than 3,500 persons; that summer, American entrepreneur Moses Austin arrives in San Antonio de Béxar to request land for American colonization in Texas; he is granted land and the privilege of recruiting 300 families to Texas the following year.
1821	Mexico gains its independence from Spain through the Mexican Revolution; Moses Austin dies in June.
1822	General Agustín de Iturbide is crowned emperor of Mexico; he proves incompetent and is driven from power, by, among others, General Antonio López de Santa Anna; Moses Austin's son, Stephen, begins colonizing lands in Texas with American families.
1824	The Mexicans establish a federal government, including a two-house legislature and an elected president; the new framework of government is the Constitution of 1824; Stephen Austin has completed 272 new land titles in Texas, nearly all to Americans.
1826	Empresarios Benjamin and Haden Edwards lead a revolt against Mexican authority and attempt to found the Republic of Fredonia; by January 1827, the rebellion has been contained by Mexican officials.
1828	Louisianian Jim Bowie arrives in Texas.
1830s	As Americans occupy Texas lands, six new villages come into existence; thousands of Americans occupy lands, mostly as farmers; as early as 1830, the lands of the empresarios are home to approximately 20,000 people.
1830	Mexican Congress passes the Decree of April 6, declaring Texas closed to further colonization by Americans; Americans continue to come to Texas illegally.
1831	Mexican governor of Coahuila, General Mier y Terán orders the arrest of Texas land officials who have granted titles to newly arrived Americans; William Travis arrives in Texas and soon becomes

involved in a "War Party" bent on pursuing the independence of Texas from Mexico.

1833 Stephen Austin travels to Mexico City to request Mexican state status for Texas; he is later jailed; that same year, Sam Houston arrives in Texas.

1835 Mexican General Santa Anna creates a puppet government in Mexico and dissolves the state legislature; he also clamps down on customs violations by Americans in Texas; the Texas Revolution kicks into high gear; Santa Anna dispatches General Cos to Texas to take control of San Antonio de Béxar and to bring the Texans back in line.

October Texans gather in convention to discuss the future of Texas; as they meet, Cos arrives in San Antonio and occupies the town; his troops are garrisoned in the old mission complex called the Alamo; later that month, Jim Bowie and about 90 Texans engage in a fight with 400 Mexican dragoons outside of San Antonio.

October 2 Texans in Gonzales fight Mexican troops to retain ownership of their "Come and Take It" cannon; the Texans win the fight, but have to abandon their cannon after its cart falls apart.

November 1 As part of the "Army of the People," Texans surround San Antonio, trapping General Cos inside.

November 3 Texas Convention delegates promise to support the Mexican Constitution of 1824, yet agree to move toward independence if the Mexican government fails to recognize the validity of the 1824 Constitution.

December 5–9 Texans storm Cos's positions in San Antonio de Béxar and inside the Alamo; Cos is forced to surrender and is ordered out of Texas.

1836

January Santa Anna marches north toward Texas and reaches Saltillo on January 7; he follows the El Camino Real, bound for San Antonio.

January 17 Sam Houston orders Jim Bowie and 30 Texans to San Antonio to destroy the old Alamo mission, which Houston believes is indefensible.

January 26 A rally is held in San Antonio, calling for the defense of the Alamo; a resolution is passed; Bowie is the second man to sign the document.

February 8 Davy Crockett arrives at the Alamo with several Tennessee associates.

February 11 William Travis gains command of the fortress of the Alamo after the previous commander, James Neill, passes it to him.

February 13	Santa Anna's army is hit by a violent snowstorm.
February 20	William Travis, co-commander at the Alamo, is informed that Santa Anna's army has crossed the Rio Grande; Santa Anna's troops are now within 50 miles of San Antonio.
February 23	Residents of San Antonio spot Santa Anna's advance troops and begin fleeing the Texas community; Texans take refuge inside the Alamo compound; the first day of a 13-day siege begins; Travis sends first couriers out to request help in defending the Alamo.
February 24	Santa Anna orders the Mexican artillery into position around the Alamo compound; Travis pens his famous "Victory or Death" letter.
February 25	Mexicans launch a limited frontal assault involving 200 to 300 troops; the attack is repulsed; Santa Anna's men try to take up positions near the Alamo in the adobe huts of La Villita; that night, the Texans burn the huts; Juan Seguín is sent out with a message to the Texans at Gonzales.
February 26	James Fannin, Texas commander at Goliad receives word of the Alamo Siege; he prepares to take 300 reinforcements to San Antonio to help his fellow Texans.
February 27	Davy Crockett may have fired his long rifle directly at Santa Anna, sending the Mexican general scurrying for cover.
February 28	Fannin abandons the rescue, facing equipment failure and a fear of leaving Goliad defenseless.
February 29	Thirty-two Texans from Gonzales arrive at the Alamo to reinforce the garrison.
March 2	Texas council at Washington-on-the-Brazos votes for independence and orders Sam Houston to take volunteers to San Antonio to rescue the Alamo defenders; Houston sets his date for departure as March 6, the day the Alamo will fall.
March 3	Santa Anna prepares to launch a full-scale attack on the Alamo compound to bring an end to the siege; that evening, a rider reaches the Alamo to inform Travis that Fannin's men are not coming.
March 4	Mexican gun emplacements have been moved as close as 250 feet (76 meters) to the Alamo walls.
March 5	Travis draws a line across the Alamo grounds, inviting all those defenders who wished to remain inside the Alamo and fight to the death to step across it; all but one man do; that evening, the Mexican army prepares for a dawn attack on the following day.

March 6	Final day of the siege of the Alamo:
12:00 A.M.	Mexican officers begin waking their men and readying them for the attack.
1:00 A.M.	The Mexican military units begin to advance.
4:00 A.M.	Most of the Mexican troops—close to 3,000 men—are in place, in four assault columns, around the perimeter of the Alamo compound.
5:00 A.M.	An unknown Mexican soldier shouts "*Viva Santa Anna!*", and a bugle call follows; the assault begins; the Texans awake and prepare to meet the attack.
6:30 A.M.	The battle for the Alamo is over; all defenders have been or soon will be killed.
Afternoon	Mexicans build pyres and burn the bodies of the Alamo defenders.
March 11	Sam Houston receives word of the fall of the Alamo and the annihilation of its defenders.
March 20	Mexican General Urrea's army captures nearly 400 Texans in Goliad.
March 27	Under orders from Santa Anna, the Goliad Texans are executed.
April 21	Texas commander Sam Houston defeats Santa Anna in the Battle of San Jacinto, bringing about recognition of Texas's independence from Mexico.

NOTES

CHAPTER 1, THE LANDS OF TEJAS
Page 11:   "country of fine appearance . . ."
T. R. Fehrenbach, *Lone Star: A History of Texas and theTexans*. New York: Macmillan Publishing Co., Inc., 1968, p. 27.

CHAPTER 2, GONE TO TEXAS
Page 25:   "I shall earn nothing . . ." David Nevin, *The Texans*. New York: TIME-Life Books, 1975, p. 19.

Page 27:   "I now can go . . ." Ibid., 24.

Page 27:   "begged me to tell . . ." Ibid.

Page 28:   "a most beautiful . . ." Ibid.

Page 29:   "No sturdy forest here . . ." Walter Lord, *A Time to Stand: The Epic of the Alamo Seen as a Great National Experience*. New York: Harper & Brothers, 1961, p. 23.

Page 29:   "It does not appear . . ." Ibid., p. 24.

Page 30:   "The sheer abundance . . ." Ibid., p. 25.

Page 31:   "I arrived in . . ." Nevin, p. 29.

Page 32:   "Moral and industrious . . ." Ibid., p. 32.

Page 33:   "No frontiersman who . . ." T. R. Fehrenbach, *Lone Star: A History of Texas and the Texans*. New York: Macmillan Publishing Co., Inc., 1968, p. 142.

Page 34:   "[They were] as good . . ." Nevin, p. 34.

Page 35:   "show me their titles . . ." Nevin, p. 38.

Page 37:   "coffee, cornbread . . ." Ibid., p. 36.

Page 37:   "brick stores and frame . . ." Ibid.

Page 37:   "clothing made in . ." Fehrenbach, p. 143.

Page 38:   "The colony was . . ." Ibid.

CHAPTER 3, A LAND OF REVOLUTION
Page 43:   "While Mexicans were . . ." T. R. Fehrenbach, *Lone Star: A History of Texas and the Texans*. New York: Macmillan Publishing Co., Inc., 1968, p. 166.

Page 45:   "moody, touchy, . . ." Walter Lord, *A Time to Stand: The Epic of the Alamo Seen as a Great National Experience*. New York: Harper & Brothers, 1961, p. 34.

Page 48:   "Texas needs . . ." Lynn I. Perrigo, *The American Southwest: Its People and Cultures*. Albuquerque: University of New Mexico Press, p. 118.

Page 50:   "This is a painful . . ." David Nevin, *The Texans*. New York: TIME-Life Books, 1975, p. 58.

Page 51:   "An eagle swooped . . ." Ibid.

Page 52:   "A successful military . . ." Ibid., pp. 66, 68.

Page 54:   "stab like a dagger . . ." Nevin, p. 60.

Page 54:   "the greatest fighter . . ." Ibid.

Page 55:   "put to the sword . . ." Lord, p. 37.

CHAPTER 4, THE TEXANS DEFEND THEMSELVES
Page 58:   "Let each man come . . ." Walter Lord, *A Time to Stand: The Epic of the Alamo Seen as a Great National Experience*. New York: Harper & Brothers, 1961, p. 41.

Page 58:   "base, unprincipled . . ." David Nevin, *The Texans*. New York: TIME-Life Books, 1975, p. 71.

Page 58:   "War is our only . . ." Lynn I. Perrigo, *The American Southwest: Its People and Cultures*. Albuquerque: University of New Mexico Press, p. 120.

Page 59:   "Buckskin breeches . . ." T. R. Fehrenbach, *Lone Star: A History of Texas and the Texans*. New York: Macmillan Publishing Co., Inc., 1968, p. 195.

Page 64:   "Boys, who will come . . ." Lord, p. 57.

Page 64:   "Then fall in line! . . ." Fehrenbach, p. 197.

Page 64:   "On the third day . . ." Ibid., p.198.

CHAPTER 5, THE SIEGE BEGINS
Page 71:   "Man is nothing . . ." David Nevin, *The Texans*. New York: TIME-Life Books, 1975, p. 64.

Page 72:   "By now the men . . ." Walter Lord, *A Time to Stand: The Epic of the Alamo Seen as a Great National Experience*. New York: Harper & Brothers, 1961, p. 72.

Page 73:   "I have ordered . . ." Jeff Long, *Duel of Eagles: The Mexican and U.S. Fight for the Alamo*. New York: William Morrow and Company, Inc., 1990, p. 119.

Page 74:   "Since we heard . . ." Ibid., p. 120.

Page 74:   "The salvation . . ." Nevin, p. 85.

Page 78:   "you may go to Hell . . ." Walter Blair, *Davy Crockett: Legendary Frontier Hero, His True Life Story and the Fabulous Tall Tales Told About Him*. Springfield, IL: Lincoln-Herndon Press, Inc., 1986, p. 120.

Page 78:   "I have taken the oath . . ." Long, p. 107.

Page 78:   "Me and my Tennessee . . ." William C. Davis, *Three Roads to the Alamo: The Lives and Fortunes of David Crockett, James Bowie, and William Barret Travis*. New York: HarperCollins Publishers, 1998, p. 516.

Page 80:   "The enemy in large . . ." Nevin, p. 96.

Page 81:   "Colonel, here am I . . ." Bill
              Groneman, *Death of a Legend: The Myth
              and Mystery Surrounding the Death of
              Davy Crockett*. Plano: Republic of Texas
              Press, 1999, p. 8.

CHAPTER 6, VICTORY OR DEATH

Page 84:   "To the People . . ." David Nevin, *The
              Texans*. New York: TIME-Life Books,
              1975, p. 98.

Page 85:   "It will be impossible . . ." Ibid.

Page 89:   "Monday, February 29 . . ." Walter
              Lord, *A Time to Stand: The Epic of
              the Alamo Seenas a Great National
              Experience*. New York: Harper &
              Brothers, 1961, p. 123.

Page 90:   "This man would . . ." Nevin, p. 101.

Page 90:   "The Hon. David . . ." William C.
              Davis, *Three Roads to the Alamo: The
              Lives and Fortunes of David Crockett,
              James Bowie, and William Barret Travis*.
              New York: HarperCollins Publishers,
              1998, p. 542.

Page 90:   "people in town . . ." Ibid., p. 545.

Page 90:   "the tejanos in Bexar . . ." Ibid.

Page 92:   "At least two hundred . . ." Nevin, pp.
              101, 103; T. R. Fehrenbach, *Lone Star:
              A History of Texas and the Texans*. New
              York: Macmillan Publishing Co., Inc.,
              1968, p. 211.

Page 94:   "march tomorrow or . . ." Lord, p. 130.

Page 95:   "Take care of my . . ." Ibid., p. 143.

Page 95:   "Let the convention . . ." Nevin, p. 103.

Page 96:   "I think we had . . ." Lord, p. 144.

Page 97:   "Finally, in an isolated . . ." Jeff Long,
              *Duel of Eagles: The Mexican and U.S.
              Fight for the Alamo*. New York: William
              Morrow and Company, Inc., 1990,
              p. 230.

Page 98:   "My brave companions . . ." Ibid., p. 232.

Page 99:   "Boys, I am not . . ." Ibid., p. 233.

Page 99:   "You may as well . . ." Ibid.

CHAPTER 7, THE MEXICANS ARE COMING

Page 102:   "Viva Santa Anna . . ." David Nevin,
              The Texans. New York: TIME-Life
              Books, 1975, p. 106.

Page 103:   "Colonel Travis . . ." Ibid.

Page 103:   "Come on boys . . ." Jeff Long, *Duel of
              Eagles: The Mexican and U.S. Fight for
              the Alamo*. New York: William Morrow
              and Company, Inc., 1990, p. 242.

Page 104-105: "The attack did not go . . ." Nevin,
              p. 106.

Page 105:   "A quarter of an hour . . ." Long,
              p. 246.

Page 107:   "He may have died . . ." William C.
              Davis, *Three Roads to the Alamo: The
              Lives and Fortunes of David Crockett,
              James Bowie, and William Barret Travis*.
              New York: HarperCollins Publishers,
              1998, p. 738, Ftn. #108.

Page 108:   "But disorder had . . ." Ibid., pp. 247–248.

Page 109:   "the arms, principally . . ." Ibid., p. 249.

Page 109:   "Great God, Sue . . ." Ibid.

Page 110:   "Thus betrayed, our men . . ." Ibid.,
              p. 251.

Page 111:   "was pierced . . ." Bill Groneman, *Death
              of a Legend: The Myth and Mystery
              Surrounding the Death of Davy Crockett*.
              Plano: Republic of Texas Press, 1999,
              p. 82.

Page 111:   "it is not a cat . . ." Long, p. 253.

Page 111:   "like a woman . . ." Ibid.

Page 111:   "tossed Bowie's body . . ." Nevin, p. 107.

Page 112:   "The enemy loss . . ." Ibid., p. 109.

Page 112:   "a small affair . . ." Ibid.

CHAPTER 8, WILL YOU COME TO THE BOWER?

Page 118:   "The most awful slaughter . . ." David
              Nevin, *The Texans*. New York: TIME-
              Life Books, 1975, p. 137.

Page 118–119: "I saw his Excellency . . ." Ibid., p. 140.

Page 119:   "That man may . . ." Ibid., p. 141.

Page 119:   "You should have . . ." Ibid.

Blair, Walter. *Davy Crockett: Legendary Frontier Hero, His True Life Story and the Fabulous Tall Tales told About Him*. Springfield, IL: Lincoln-Herndon Press, Inc., 1986.

Davis, William C. *Three Roads to the Alamo: The Lives and Fortunes of David Crockett, James Bowie, and William Barret Travis*. New York: HarperCollins Publishers, 1998.

De La Pena, José Enrique, and Carmen Perry. *With Santa Anna in Texas: A Personal Narrative of the Revolution*. College Station: Texas A&M University Press, 1997.

Edmonson, J. R. *The Alamo Story: From Early History to Current Conflicts*. Plano: Republic of Texas Press, 2000.

Fehrenbach, T. R. *Lone Star: A History of Texas and the Texans*. New York: Macmillan Publishing Company, 1968.

Garland, Sherry. *In the Shadow of the Alamo*. San Diego: Harcourt, 2001.

Groneman, Bill. *Death of a Legend: The Myth and Mystery Surrounding the Death of Davy Crockett*. Plano: Republic of Texas Press, 1999.

———. *Eyewitness to the Alamo*. Plano, TX: Wordware Publishing, Inc., 2001.

Hardin, Stephen. *The Alamo 1836: Crockett's Last Stand*. New York: Osprey Publishing, 2001.

Harrigan, Stephen. *The Gates of the Alamo*. New York: Alfred A. Knopf, 2000.

Hoyt, Edwin Palmer. *The Alamo: An Illustrated History*. Dallas: Taylor Publishing, 1999.

Long, Jeff. *Duel of Eagles: The Mexican and U.S. Fight for the Alamo*. New York: William Morrow and Company, Inc., 1990.

Lord, Walter. *A Time to Stand: The Epic of the Alamo Seen as a Great National Experience*. New York: Harper & Brothers, 1961.

Nevin, David. *The Texans*. New York: TIME-Life Books, 1975.

Nofi, Albert A. *Alamo and the Texas War of Independence: Heroes, Myths, and History*. New York: Da Capo Press, Incorporated, 2001.

Olson, James N. *Line in the Sand: The Alamo in Blood and Memory*. New York: The Free Press, 2000.

Perrigo, Lynn I. *The American Southwest: Its People and Cultures*. Albuquerque: University of New Mexico Press, 1971.

Tinkle, Lon. *13 Days to Glory: The Siege of the Alamo*. College Station: Texas A&M University Press, 1996.

Bredeson, Carmen. *The Battle of the Alamo: The Fight for Texas Territory*. Brookfield, CT: Millbrook Press, 1996.

Gaines, Ann Graham. *Jim Bowie: Hero of the Alamo*. Springfield, NJ: Enslow Publishers Inc., 2000.

Garland, Sherry. *Voices of the Alamo*. Danbury, CT: Scholastic, Inc., 2000.

Huffines, Alan C. *Blood of Noble Men: The Alamo Siege and Battle*. Austin: Eakin Press, 1999.

Jakes, T. D. *Susanna of the Alamo: A True Story*. San Diego: Harcourt, 1990.

Kilgore, Dan. *How Did Davy Die?* College Station: Texas A&M University Press, 1978.

Love, D. Anne. *I Remember the Alamo*. New York: Bantam Doubleday Dell Books for Young Readers, 1996.

Santella, Andrew. *The Battle of the Alamo*. Danbury, CT: Children's Press, 1997.

Warner, Gertrude Chandler. *The Mystery of the Alamo*. (The Boxcar Children Series) Morton Grove, IL: Albert Whitman, 1997.

TIM MCNEESE is an Associate Professor of History at York College in Nebraska. He is the author of more than fifty books and educational materials on everything from Egyptian pyramids to American Indians. Professor McNeese graduated from York College with his Associate of Arts degree, as well as Harding University where he received his Bachelor of Arts degree in history and political science. He received his Master of Arts degree in history from Southwest Missouri State University. His audiences range from elementary students to adults. He is currently in his 27th year of teaching. Professor McNeese's writing career has earned him a citation in the "Something About the Author" reference work. He is married to Beverly McNeese who teaches English at York College.